Process and Portfolios in Writing Instruction

Process and Portfolios in Writing Instruction

Classroom Practices in Teaching English
Vol. 26

Kent Gill, Editor,
and the Committee on Classroom Practices

National Council of Teachers of English
1111 W. Kenyon Road, Urbana, Illinois 61801-1096

Cover Design: R. Maul

Interior Design: Doug Burnett

Production Editor: Michelle Sanden Johlas

Manuscript Editors: Humanities & Sciences Associates

NCTE Stock Number: 37245–3050

Library of Congress Catalog Card Number 85–644740

Contents

Introduction

T he past two decades have seen a revolution in the teaching of writing. The changes have been incremental and gradual—as practicing teachers, Writing Project programs, university professors, and NCTE committees have tried new methods, evaluated them, refined and shared them—but the effect really has been quite revolutionary. The writing process approach to writing instruction that resulted has created a very different, much improved environment in which young people learn the skills of written communication.

The writing teachers of 1973 assigned topics, set due dates, and waited for the papers to come in. Prior instruction might have included the topic outline or the five-paragraph format. Grammar instruction in parts of speech and types of sentences was intended to prepare the students to produce acceptable prose. Direct spelling instruction was assumed to transfer to the students' written work. The teachers may have sympathized with the many students who experienced writer's block, but they had few tools to offer for breaking it. Then the papers came in and had to be marked, with every error noted, long into the night. The teachers finally assigned letter grades, which were duly recorded.

The writing teachers of 1993, however, come armed with a wide range of prewriting strategies that can help students build ideas and vocabulary for a writing activity. After writing in journals, clustering, brainstorming, mapping, and word-banking, few writers can honestly say they do not have anything to write about. An organic instructional theory relates grammatical, structural, and technical matters to the immediate and direct needs of the writers; teaching becomes oriented to the problems the writers are encountering. Students are encouraged to be sensitive to their audience, to think through their purposes, to write in an honest, real voice. Students also work through multiple drafts, learning revision strategies and editing skills in the course of working toward a final draft. At all stages they may use cooperative learning activities to support one another.

Instead of the interminable marking of papers, the writing instructors of 1993 are responding to writers, acting as advisors and critics, modeling the behavior of the writers by being writers themselves, alongside their students. The development of the portfolio idea enables the teacher to use a sampling technique to evaluate students' progress in writing ability. Judging student portfolios against a set of criteria enables the portfolio to contribute to program assessment.

We can demonstrate the influence of this revolutionary approach to writing instruction by presenting, here, a set of essays offered by practicing teachers, drawn from and tested in their classrooms. We find teachers refining the steps in the process of writing by applying creativity and good judgment. We also find that teachers' experiences with the portfolio assert the importance of the achievement. Ultimately, we discover a sea of change in the way students are taught to write—a change for the better.

Kent Gill
Camp Sherman, Oregon

I Writing: From Motivation to Revision

Today's teachers have at their disposal a vastly augmented methodology for teaching writing. They can utilize tested writing-process approaches, developing rich prewriting activities: clustering, mapping, brainstorming. They can follow up with a variety of revision strategies: peer-group responses, multiple drafts, portfolios. Nonetheless, the teaching of writing continues to pose problems for them. They worry about motivation, they deal with reluctant writers, they meet children from non-English-language backgrounds. They have large classes, composed of students of differing abilities, with varied interests. Therefore, they seek teaching methods that will enable them to help each of these students become comfortable and competent in writing.

Teachers are looking for assistance. To provide that assistance, we follow, in this first section of the book, the accounts of a group of English teachers who have found some particular success in teaching students to write.

In "Images," Gail M. Young describes a project for helping reluctant writers over the hurdle of not having anything to say. A directive prewriting activity with an important graphic component leads her students to success with poetic imagery.

Facing a similar problem of students stymied by writer's block, Robert W. Keiper, in "Scavenger Hunt," reports how a field trip to a nearby urban center provided a wealth of material which his student writers subsequently crafted into a series of written pieces.

In "Life Maps," Beverly Wilkins and Betty McWilliams describe how they collaborated in using Dan Kirby's concept of a "life map" to help their students draw upon a body of material from their own lives, ideas they could use for writing.

Three reports from the college level explore how to get teachers to see themselves as writers. In "They Said I Was an Author," Robert J.

Nistler shows how he involved teachers in learning about the writing process from the inside, as writers themselves. He follows these teachers as they learn to relish their writing experience, noting their observations about what was happening in their process journals.

Lela M. DeToye, in "Writing a Student Profile," details how her college students interviewed primary schoolchildren about their experiences in acquiring language skills and then wrote up these interviews as first-person profiles, using the voice of the child.

D. R. Ransdell, in "Teachers as Writers," shows how she shared her own experience in revising a magazine article with her college class, both to motivate the students' revision efforts and to demonstrate how they might do it.

Elaine Murphy used a different approach for making revision accessible to students. In "Group Paragraphs: A Route to Revision," she shows how a group-written essay can generate sound revision practices that students can apply to their own work.

In "Glossing: A Revision Technique," Marylyn E. Calabrese describes how her students used marginal notes, written to the teacher, to describe and justify the changes they made during revision.

1 Images

Gail M. Young
Hillsboro High School, Hillsboro, Oregon

Student: "How much do we have to write?"
Young: "One well-developed paragraph . . . about 100 to 150 words."
Student: "I CAN'T WRITE THAT MUCH!!!!!"
Young: "Well, write for about twenty minutes."
Student: "TWENTY MINUTES!!!!!!!"
Young: "Well, then . . . try just a few words."

Inspiration and Rationale

Project "Images" was inspired by nearly two decades of teaching students whom we, in the profession, refer to as reluctant learners. The project was piloted using a group of thirty special education students who exhibited learning disabilities, specifically deficits in written expression and/or language. Because they lacked skills and knew it, these students felt inadequate and avoided writing of any kind. For them, an assignment that required "just a few words" was the least troublesome of writing tasks, so I decided that poetry, with its economy of words, would be the genre best suited to their writing abilities. However, because "poetry," like many terms, sometimes suffers from negative connotations, I never used the term itself—instead, we would be writing "Images"!

Description and Purpose

"Images," a six-week project designed to encourage and direct reluctant writers in the poetic experience, involved a series of five prompts that provided both the stimulus and structure for the writing process. Students in the project had the opportunity to share their writing with classmates at several stages, and ultimately, to see their favorite pieces published in a collection entitled, appropriately enough, *IMAGES.*

The Process

I used each of the five prompts for a two-day lesson, taught in twenty- to thirty-minute segments over two consecutive days. A different prompt was used each week, for five weeks, and the order of the prompts was arbitrary; in fact, there is no element of exclusivity attached to any of the five.

On the first day of each prompt, a Thursday, students were given a prompt handout on which to gather (prewrite) raw material, the ingredients for the next day's writing. Group brainstorming sometimes helped the students who had trouble generating ideas; sometimes I modeled this step by thinking out loud in response to a prompt, so that the students could observe me in the prewriting step.

On Friday, I returned the prompt sheets, passed out blank paper, and provided a "creativity environment." The prewriting and writing steps were separated by one day to give fuller attention to day one's planning stage and also to ensure each writer a fresh mind and better concentration for day two's creative efforts. An additional advantage that I discovered was that students frequently played with and worked over their ideas, arriving on day two "ready to write."

The "creativity environment" had two features: it was an interruption-free time (all questions and comments had to come before); and it contained what I called "creativity music" (anything without lyrics: classical, jazz, whatever), which signaled the start of, and continued throughout the creative writing time.

I explained to the students that, given the raw material from the previous day's prompt and the creativity environment they were working in, magic would happen. And, in fact, it often did!

Revisions

Revisions were made at several steps throughout the writing process. Many students were eager to read their "images" as soon as creativity time ended. When they heard the "sound" of their own pieces, they often made changes. Comments from classmates—such as "Your last line is confusing," "You should describe that better," "You used that word too many times"—inspired reconsideration in other students.

On Monday came another opportunity for revision. I returned images which I had proofread for spelling and typed out in a poetic format. Students were pleased to see their work look so "official," as one class member put it. They read again, but this time with revision in mind. A few more students read pieces to the class, while others chose to fine-tune the language of their own writing. My students usually lacked motivation to revise their work, but during Project Images, revision occurred more often and more purposefully than in any other writing activity I had led.

Selection

At the end of the fifth week, most of the students had five images to reread, evaluate, and consider for publication. In most cases, they knew quickly which two were their favorites. However, some students did not like any of the pieces they had written, but a few could not discard any! At this point the importance of audience became obvious. Undecided students read pieces for audience response; even students who felt certain of their choices wanted to participate in our poetry reading. Selections were made, and we were off to press!

The Five Weekly Prompts

Prompt One: Word Chain

"Word chain" is the prompt I used both as a review of the parts of speech and as a means of generating a wide variety of words for use in the creative process. First, students focused on a topic about which they knew something or had strong feelings. Then I asked them to think about the four categories "chained" below that topic. "Describe it" generated some vivid adjectives; "What it's like" tapped the notion of similes and metaphors; verbs and adverbs for "action" and "how" rounded out the word pool. After students chose a topic (some brainstorming was necessary at this point), I modeled by choosing "aerobics" and completing the prompt. Then students word-chained their own topics. On day two, when they wrote their images, they fleshed out their ideas, selecting, adding, deleting (figure 1).

Prompt Two: Opposites

For "opposites," an exercise in using contrast for emphasis, I instructed the students to write word opposites on either side of a diagonal line. This prompt relied heavily on group brainstorming, as students gathered the ingredients for their image writing. The students, in a verbal free-for-all, suggested opposites; I wrote the pairs on the board so that their choices would not be limited by spelling. They could include any that appealed to them, or they could write their own without sharing, if they chose to be independent. Day two opened with an individual selection of three or four pairs of words. The creativity environment was established, and the students began to write images (figure 2).

Prompt Three: Favorite Letter

Alliteration and euphony as poetic devices were the motivation for "favorite letter." Students chose a letter and listed thirty to forty words that begin with it. This prompt resulted in the most fun, with a number of students slipping into silliness. Many chose the initial of their first name, which added to the personality and voice of the piece. On day two, the students faced their entire list of words. I explained that, of course, they would not use all of the words and that they would have to add connecting words. One student asked how they would know which words to write. I replied that when the music began and he was focused on the creative process, he would know; it would happen. It did (figure 3).

Prompt Four: Even More

This prompt was my attempt to use comparatives and superlatives as vehicles for expressing emotion and energy. I asked students to respond to five open-ended statements: "I hate it when . . . "; "I'm angry when . . . "; "I'm happy when . . . "; "I'm sad when . . . "; and "I like it when . . . ." After the five situations were defined, I asked students to choose the one that hit them most strongly. For this one emotional experience, I encouraged them to think in the comparative and superlative by completing the appropriate variation of the two phrases: "I hate it even more when . . . " and "But I hate it the most when . . . ." On day two, some students used two or three of their emotional responses, which had not been my intent; nonetheless, those images were as powerful and appealing as the ones which focused on a single emotion (figure 4).

Prompt Five: Confusion

The prompt which elicited the most energy was "confusion." The format of the prompt paper required the students to literally write in circles as they turned their papers to record a situation which confused them. Later, several commented that they actually felt a bit dizzy as they rotated their papers to read to the class! In preparation, I modeled the prompt by verbalizing a student's thoughts when faced with a math story problem: "I know how to add, subtract, multiply, and divide, but I don't know which to do when I see all those numbers. In fact, I don't

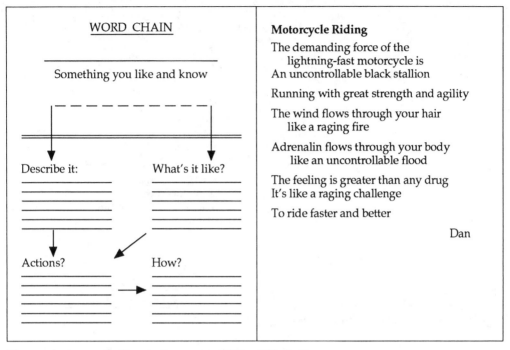

Figure 1. Image written to the prompt "Word Chain."

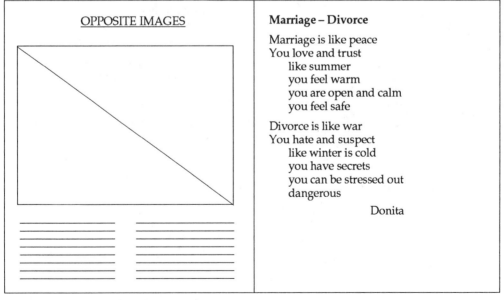

Figure 2. Image written to the prompt "Opposites."

FAVORITE LETTER

List words:

Secrets of the Solar System

Solar system
Soundless
Sightful
always Seeking
probes Scouting.

full of stars as suns
sad, lonely
seems to be no life.

Others will look at SATURN
full of sulfur, methane,
Ring and nine satellites
Asteroids scatter throughout
the Solar system.

The Solar system holds Secrets
that soon will be Solved
Maybe some day.

                                                    Nate

Figure 3. Image written to the prompt "Favorite Letter."

EVEN MORE

I hate it when:
I'm angry when:
I'm happy when:
I'm sad when:
I like it when:

Even more when:

But the most when:

People and Happiness

Happiness is different for everyone
For some it's a smile
And others, it may be a big box of candy.

That's what makes everyone different

Happiness can come in so many ways
You may think it's gone and
You think you could never see it again,
Next thing you know

        You have that same smile
        or box of candy.

                                                    Tiffanie

Figure 4. Image written to the prompt "Even More."

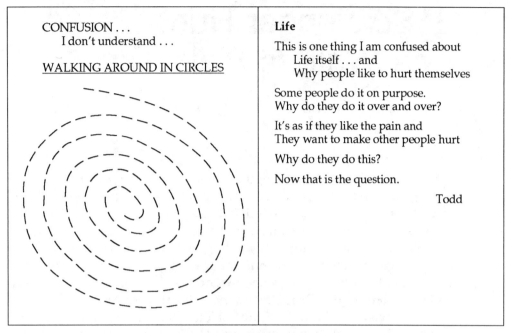

CONFUSION . . .
   I don't understand . . .

<u>WALKING AROUND IN CIRCLES</u>

Life

This is one thing I am confused about
   Life itself . . . and
   Why people like to hurt themselves

Some people do it on purpose.
Why do they do it over and over?

It's as if they like the pain and
They want to make other people hurt

Why do they do this?

Now that is the question.

                                    Todd

Figure 5. Image written to the prompt "Confusion."

even know which numbers to use!" They could certainly relate to this situation. On day two, the writing for this prompt was more straightforward than for other prompts because most students had already written the image. They simply adapted the format to their words (figure 5).

Analysis of the Prompts

After we published and enjoyed our images, and took pleasure in the surprised expressions of our very impressed readers, I analyzed the success of the five prompts on the basis of which ones had been selected for our publication. Twenty-nine students had chosen two images, and there were fifty-eight pieces in the collection. The breakdown by prompts was as follows: word chain = ten images; opposites = fifteen images; favorite letter = nine images; even more = fifteen images; and confusion = eight images. That's fifty-seven in all. One image was written in class one day while I was teaching a totally different lesson. That one was prompted, I suspect, by *boredom*!

2 Scavenger Hunt: A Writer's Field Trip

Robert W. Keiper
Western Washington University

One of the most challenging aspects of teaching composition is formulating topics for student writing—topics which are interesting, enjoyable, and educational for writer and reader alike. Many assignments can become trite and predictable; consequently, the teacher ends up spending hours toiling through compositions that exhibit little in the way of new thought or imagination. These papers are written under duress and follow a standard plan, i.e., "Read the story and explain the symbolism, the theme, the nature of Man . . . "

"Scavenger Hunt: A Writer's Field Trip" is one activity I have developed that not only makes formulating topics easy, but also provides students with an exercise in honing their observation skills. From the collection process of the field trip, students obtain a wealth of information and ideas that enable them to write essays, short stories, poetry, and dramatic scripts. The range of assignments and activities generated from the "scavenger hunt" is limited only by the imagination, ambition, and daring of the students and the teacher.

The idea came to me when I grew weary of hearing the proverbial "I don't know what to write!" or "I don't know anything to write about!" while teaching sophomore English. What we seemed to need was a collection activity, something to furnish the students with a full load of information. The activity would also need to provide a wide range of compositions approaches, thus avoiding the predictability of most assignments.

Through an interest inventory and polling of the class, we discovered that the majority of the students had never been downtown to the heart of the city. Our particular school was one of four high schools in a large suburban setting, some twelve miles from the city center. The school had an enrollment of 1,800 students in grades 9–12, with a low to middle socioeconomic makeup. The student body was culturally and ethnically diverse. Few students had ventured downtown and experienced the beauty and ugliness, the people and rhythms of the city. An excursion into the city seemed to offer a splendid collection opportunity: students would have to use all of their senses for accumulating information.

The old game of a scavenger hunt became the focus of how the students would gather information they could use later in writing. Since cost was an important factor, we decided to use the public transit system: this would be the most inexpensive means of transportation, and would provide the students with excellent opportunities for completing a portion of the scavenger hunt list on their way downtown. (Many students considered this a major event, since they had never ridden a public bus.) The students needed only bus fare and money for lunch, so the school had to cover only the cost of a substitute teacher.

Prior to field-trip day, class time was devoted to interpreting bus schedules, reading and marking maps, and researching facts and features of the city. Teams of two to three students developed sample scavenger items. The students also worked cooperatively in formulating the strategies and rules for the scavenger hunt. They decided that the teams would not see the actual lists until they were on the bus; the instructor would be the only one who knew the items on each list; a three-hour time limit would be set for meeting back at the bus stop once downtown; and the prize for the best team effort and collection would be a day off from class.

The following list provides a sample of the types of information found on the students' lists:

1. List two things that will be in the same place 10 years, 100 years, 1,000 years from today. (State the exact location and give reasons for their stability.)

2. List five things that will be gone tomorrow. (State the exact location and who or what will remove them.)

3. Describe in detail an eyesore. (State the exact location and why the team believes it is an eyesore.)

4. Describe in detail something useless. (Why is it of no use to the team? Who or what might find it useful?)

5. Describe something that needs repair. (How would the team fix it?)

6. Describe something that is being repaired. (How is it being repaired from the team's perspective?)

7. Find at least three examples of a poetic sign, bumper sticker, graffiti, slogan, or advertisement. (What does it say? Does it use imagery, irony, symbolism? Why did it get the team's attention?)

8. Describe in detail a unique individual. (If the team feels comfortable, follow the person for a few minutes, noticing the person's walk, dress, attitude, and gestures. Make up an identity for the individual, i.e., name, family, occupation, education, etc., and attempt a sketch of this individual.)

9. Sketch the most unique building.

10. Sketch the most intriguing/interesting sight other than a human or an animal.

11. Relate/describe examples of kindness, proper etiquette, or caring illustrated by individuals.

12. Relate/describe examples of rudeness or uncaring.

13. Describe a truly bizarre sight, smell, or feeling.

14. Ask four people for directions to a specific location; check their accuracy and how they communicated the instructions, i.e., body movement, vocal intonation, facial expressions, etc.

15. Sit for ten to fifteen minutes in one spot and list all the sounds, smells, feelings, sights, and "tastes" of that location. (Give exact location.)

16. Interview a police officer, valet parking attendant, street cleaner, vendor, street person, hotel door captain, etc. (Formulate some team questions beforehand.)

The students were also given guidelines for possible compositions and assignments that would utilize the information they collected. These guidelines for writing were provided to assist the teams in using their time wisely and to guide their observations so that they would derive maximum benefit for follow-up work in class. They included the following items:

1. *Narrative Essay:* Include personal feelings, impressions, attitudes about the day, the people, the city.

2. *Sensory Images:* Utilizing all the senses, write a descriptive essay about the city for someone who has never experienced an urban area.

3. *Steps in a Process:* Compose a paper speculating on how something is being accomplished or built step-by-step.

4. *Comparison/Contrast:* What are the differences and similarities between the city and your area: the people, daily activities, rhythm, lifestyle, etc.

5. *Short Story:* Several teams combine, and as a group, share the various "characters" they witnessed and formulate a plot using the people and places they observed. Write and illustrate a short story collaboratively.

6. *Drama:* Same as #5, but collaborate on writing a one-act play with all the dramatic elements. Perform the play in class.

7. *Cause and Effect:* Examine a problem viewed by the team and state the cause of the problem and its effects on the city and/ or its people.

8. *Research:* Take either the problem in #7 or a new topic and expand it into a research paper, finding sources to support the thesis.

9. *Persuasive Writing:* Similar to #7 and #8, but take a stand on an issue and persuade the reader to take action.

10. *Poetic Interpretation:* Take the sights, sounds, feelings, and rhythms encountered in the city and put the impressions into poetic form.

Initially, this first group of students was somewhat hesitant to participate in the field trip. However, on the bus ride home, they filled the time with one-upmanship stories and shared their reflections on the day. The scavenger hunt became a tremendous motivator in course enrollment, it developed student enjoyment of writing, and it provided me with an entire school year's worth of material for compositions. The students never again uttered, "I don't have anything to write about!"

With a little creative effort by the instructor, the scavenger hunt can be adapted easily to any locale. The idea has been applied to a walking tour of the neighborhood around a school and redesigned to focus on the gathering of the history of a small town. Other teachers have adapted the scavenger hunt idea for their own courses, not only for English but for photography, art history, theatre, and science. With adaptation, creativity, and a willingness to try something different, the idea seems to provide an extraordinary, experiential learning activity that students find valuable.

3 Life Maps: A Road to Writing

Beverly Wilkins
Midway Middle School, Waco, Texas

Betty McWilliams
Waco High School, Waco, Texas

Have you ever started writing something and then realized that you just didn't like what you had written? Imagine how our students must feel when we force them to continue working on a piece of writing they just don't like. Portfolio writing is one way to solve this problem. According to Dan Kirby, writing workshop leader and author of *Inside Out* (1981), portfolio writing allows students to begin several pieces on a given subject and then select the one they feel most comfortable with to develop into a longer piece of writing.

Narrative writing, in particular, can be easily adapted to the portfolio format. One way of doing so is to use what Kirby refers to as a "life map." The map stimulates writing and provides material for several writing assignments. Following are a series of lessons we developed around Kirby's life map idea. These activities can be assigned on consecutive days or scattered across a longer time period.

Getting Started

Students are asked to create a "life map" based on their own lives. On a sheet of paper, they draw or paste pictures which illustrate their lives. The "road" on each map represents a student's personal chronology. If students need help, suggestions such as the following can be provided on the board:

friends	enemies	school experiences
travels	embarrassing moments	jobs
conflicts	foods (likes and dislikes)	toys
relatives	accomplishments	chores
accidents	births or deaths	firsts (love, date)
pets	traumatic experiences	

Some students may want to add a three-dimensional aspect to their map by pasting small mementos on it. Even young children can be guided through this process. The teacher's own life map can be used as a model.

Students then share their maps (figure 1) in small groups, commenting on a few of the items they have included. Maps can be displayed throughout the room, and then stored in the students' writing portfolios.

Writing Assignment #1 (W1)

Find an interesting short narrative or a portion of a longer one, and read it to the students, pointing out what makes the passage a narrative. You can use anything ranging from Lucy Maud Montgomery's *Anne of Green Gables* to a current murder mystery. Then have the students select an occasion illustrated on their life maps to write about in narrative form. (You may need to remind them that it must tell a story.) At this point, they should concentrate on getting their ideas down on paper, rather than using proper grammar and spelling. The narratives are usually not complete at this point, which is all right. After the students have written for a predetermined amount of time—possibly ten to thirty minutes—they should read their work aloud to a peer-response group. (These groups should be encouraged to make positive comments about each student's writing.) They could use the following questions to guide their responses:

1. What are three strong points about this narrative?
2. What, if anything, is unclear about this narrative?
3. What do you, as the reader, want to know more about?
4. What are some suggestions for improvement? (Remember, be kind and encouraging.)

Writing Assignment #2 (W2)

Follow the same instructions as in W1. You may want to continue reading from the same narrative example as before or from a different one. The students should be encouraged to select another item from their life map as the stimulus for a second narrative piece. They should not continue working on W1. Do not forget the response groups! W2 should

Figure 1. Student life map.

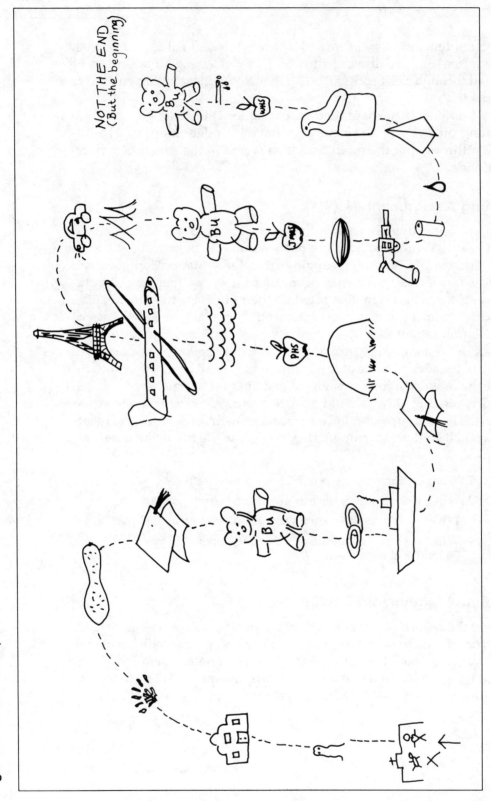

then be placed in each student's portfolio.

Writing Assignment #3 (W3)

Writing a story from someone else's point of view is a demanding experience for most students. But if your students have time to do only one writing assignment from the life map, this is the one they should do. First, read aloud an example of writing from an unusual point of view. Older students might enjoy an excerpt from John Gardner's *Grendel*, where the encounter between Beowulf and Grendel is told from the monster's point of view. Another story which is good for younger as well as older students is Jon Scieszka's *The True Story of the Three Little Pigs by A. Wolf*. This is the familiar tale of the three little pigs, but told from the wolf's point of view.

After discussing point of view with the students, instruct them to select an episode from their life map and tell it from a point of view other than their own. Some students might even enjoy writing the narrative from the point of view of an object, like a baby bottle, or from an animal's point of view. One student, Robert, wrote a moving story about deer hunting, his favorite sport, from the deer's point of view. The first paragraph follows:

> I walked a little closer, and it was there. Man, the faint smell of man. It had been a long day and I had hoped those three men and their crude form of transportation had left the pastures of my home. I was hungry so I decided to cross the dry creek bed, to a pasture on the other side. I took a quick look around and a sniff or two and nobody was in sight, so I carefully walked out of the treeline which ran along the creek. When I was clear from the protection of the trees, I noticed a noise in the distance. It was the sound of buck horns clashing and grunts from the mighty bulls fighting for a mate. It was then that the familiar scent came to me. It was him, the haunting smell of man. I darted back to the treeline and circled around and came out again. I looked around and sniffed the soft gentle breeze. Nothing. Again I could hear the noises of the mighty bucks fighting. I went a little further into the luscious green field. Then I heard a voice. It was Scotty, an old black squirrel who was captured in Scotland and sent to a zoo here in Texas, but had escaped.

After they have written their point-of-view stories, the students should read them aloud to their response groups. Then they should label their stories and place them in their portfolios.

Writing Assignment #4 (W4)

Students now select one of their writings (W1, W2, or W3) from their portfolios to develop into a polished narrative paper (W4). As a sample of a developed paper, read a narrative you have written from your life map. Students should develop their narratives by creating an interesting beginning, inserting dialogue, and adding a conclusion that shows what was learned from the experience, how it affected the writer, or what could be done differently the next time. At this point they may need lessons in punctuating dialogue, using action verbs, or writing vivid description.

Students should then share their narratives with their response groups. At this point, a written response should prove helpful to the students in revising their rough drafts.

Conclusion

We found several advantages in using the life maps to teach narrative writing: students appreciated having the chance to develop stories from their own lives; the writers also benefited from having time to let their writings "simmer" in their minds before selecting a piece for development and polishing; the portfolio format encouraged students to write more and decreased the number of assignments the teachers had to grade; by reading their work aloud to their classmates, many students discovered their own errors; and by sharing with others, a bond between classmates developed when they discovered they had similar problems. (This type of writing, when developed into a portfolio, is especially good to use at the beginning of the term or in any situation where students do not know their classmates very well.) Several of our students worked many hours outside of class revising their stories on the school's computers to submit to writing contests and to the school literary magazine. What more can teachers ask for than students who work willingly on their writing outside of class?

Work Cited

Kirby, Dan. 1981. *Inside Out: Developmental Strategies for Teaching Writing.* Upper Montclair, NJ: Boynton/Cook.

4 They Said I Was an Author

Robert J. Nistler
University of North Texas

I have become increasingly concerned with teachers' confusion about carrying out a writing process approach in their classrooms. I have found teachers willing to learn *about* writing processes, yet reluctant to *experience* writing themselves. Here, I will share a broad-based writing assignment that I have found effective for involving classroom teachers in an exploration of their own writing processes. I have found that insights derived from such involvement help teachers gain a better understanding of what may be needed in student writing programs.

The Task

The current version of this activity has evolved over several years of teaching undergraduate and graduate language arts methods courses. It has been shaped by students, colleagues, and, of course, my own teachers. The description in figure 1 was included on the syllabus for one of my recent graduate-level language arts methods courses, which met four days per week for five weeks during the summer of 1991.

When I described this portion of the syllabus during the first class period, students were visibly affected. The shifting and darting of nervous eyes led me to believe that most of the twenty-nine teachers in the class felt uneasy about having to write. As one teacher later wrote, "When I first heard about the assignment, I thought, 'Great, we'll probably have to read it out loud, too.'" Another shared her doubts by writing, "My first thoughts when this assignment was given were: 'I can't write. I've never been a good writer.'"

The teachers were unable to disguise their discomfort as I continued to explain the assignment. When I informed them that the final twenty-five minutes of each day would be used for writing, audible groans were heard. I also asked them to bring to the next class one file folder to serve as a repository for all work related to their compositions. I then explained that during the "writing workshop," I would be

Writing Experience Project

Although we seldom talk about how we write or what happens to us while we write, there is a good bit of evidence that writing is a messy business. The purpose of this assignment is to give you an opportunity to examine closely the "messy business" of your own writing process.

This paper has two parts: (1) develop a composition based on one of the weekly writing topics or one of your own choosing; and, (2) chronicle your engagement in writing processes throughout the development of your piece with a detailed description, analysis, and reflection about those processes.

You will need to include your final copy of the composition and the description of what you did and what you thought from the moment you began thinking about the composition. Include specifics—information about when you did what, where you were, the feelings that you had, who you talked with and what they said, what you read, etc. Within your description of the process you went through to write the composition, analyze what happened and reflect on what you learned about yourself and writing. See examples.

Figure 1. Instructions for the writing experience project.

writing for a portion of the time and would be using the remainder of the period to learn about them and their writing.

The Suggested Topics

During the first class meeting, I read an excerpt from Natalie Babbit's *Tuck Everlasting*. I selected a passage in which Babbit provides the reader with insights into the Tuck family by describing in great detail the appearance of the interior of the Tuck home. Following the reading, we engaged in a discussion of what we were able to surmise about the Tucks from Babbit's description. I guided our discussion so that we concluded it might be interesting for us to try to replicate Babbit's technique and write about ourselves through a description of our homes. This served as our initial writing topic. Of course, the option to write about some other topic was also provided.

Additional topics were suggested over the next two weeks. On the last day of week one, I suggested, "My Most Memorable Elementary School Language Arts Experience." During week three we considered the topic, "Myself as a Writer." In both instances, I shared papers that previous students had written on these topics.

Teachers responded to the suggested topics in a variety of ways. For some, the provision of a topic was initially overwhelming. A kindergarten teacher later wrote:

When the assignment was made to write about our most memorable language arts experience, an uneasy feeling engulfed me. Before this class, I never considered myself a writer—good or bad. Writing was a chore to wade through in order to get a grade. So I was not eager to begin the process.

Other writers, such as this fourth-grade teacher, immediately responded to a topic suggestion: "When the first topic was given, I knew that it wouldn't matter what topics would come later, I could write novels about my house." And yet others were able to move beyond suggested topics to write about what was of greater importance to them. A first-grade teacher reflected:

> I never really considered myself a good writer, although it was always easy for me to write sentimental passages on Hallmark cards. I feel that I write at my best when the topic is about something that is really dear and close to my heart. I felt like I could really let loose and write freely when I finally chose to write about my grandfather.

The Process

From the outset of the writing workshop, I wanted to write with my students and model the teacher's role during conferences. Typically, I wrote for the first five minutes of the workshop. Occasionally, I would share my compositions, in both rough and more polished stages. In addition, I made other samples of my creative writing available for the teachers' perusal. During the initial days of our writing, I mostly conducted roving conferences. I would sit next to a teacher and ask how she was doing. Next, I would ask if she would like to share her composition. If so, she would read her paper, I would comment positively, and then turn the conference back to the writer by asking for concerns or questions regarding her draft.

After two days of initiating conferences, I urged writers to share their work with those seated near them. In some cases, this meant using what I knew about a specific individual and his or her writing to match that person with a compatible partner. The result of one of these "arranged" conferences is described by a fifth-grade teacher:

> I did not read my paper again until you and I conferenced the next day during writing time. My paper was very descriptive, but it had no feeling. Your suggestion to share my writing with Ginny [a classmate] really helped me. We read our papers to each other, and I noticed that Ginny's contained a great self-

realization about what is really important to her. She suggested that I include some of my feelings toward my baby since the paper seemed to revolve around him. I shared my new draft [after another day of writing] with Ginny, Meghan, and Eugenia. Ginny and Eugenia said it sounded great, and Meghan got tears in her eyes.

By urging teachers to open conversations with colleagues at an early stage of the workshop, the development of a community of writers was fostered. In addition, as the teachers exercised greater control over the "when" and "with whom" of their conferences, my interactions with them changed. I no longer initiated conferences. Instead, the writers came to my table to share and to receive feedback on their writing.

All the teachers responded well to peer conferences. In addition to our writing and conferencing, the content discussed in class helped us analyze, question, inform, and celebrate what was occurring in our writing workshop. We always tried to connect our work with classroom practice.

During the third week of class, it became apparent that the teachers needed to share their writing with a wider audience than those seated in their particular areas. I distributed three sign-up sheets for the author's chair. Each sheet contained four spaces, one for each day of class the following week. In effect, three writing support groups of eight to ten members were created. I made clear to them that they were not required to participate as readers in the author's chair, and if they signed up, it was all right to change their minds later. Eventually, all the teachers did exercise the option to participate as readers. In describing their feelings about the author's chair, two teachers, kindergarten and fourth-grade, respectively, reported what they experienced while sharing their compositions. Feelings such as these were held in common by most of the writers:

> A few days later [after a conference with the instructor] I read my story during the Author's Chair. I will admit I was very nervous and unsure about what I had written. I felt that I had done the best that I could do, but I wondered how the writing would be accepted. Everyone made such kind remarks and was so supportive. The feeling was wonderful, and I felt so good about what I had accomplished. I came to the realization that I could write if it truly came from my heart.

> In our secluded group I did something I've never done. I orally shared an original piece of writing that was not based on research. I bared my soul. Others listened politely and then complimented me on my product. They said that I was an author. No one had ever called me an author. I was so proud.

The final week of the workshop was spent in continued polishing and sharing of compositions. Often, teachers were approached by classmates who had heard favorable comments from others about a particular composition. Typically, the result of such "favorable press" was a request for a reading of the paper. We were maturing rapidly into a true writing community.

Products

The variety of writing styles displayed, the topics explored, and the overall quality of writing alternately brought surprise, tears, laughter, and ultimately, respect. The following excerpt from one paper was inspired by the Babbit passage. Written by a first-grade teacher, this response to the first part of the "writing experience project" is representative of the kinds of compositions produced:

> As the sun begins to set upon the frontier, the image of the Indian and Cowboy atop their horses, nose to nose, on the edge of the canyon is a spectacular sight. One sits bareback, tall and proud, with bow and arrow in hand. His long, braided, charcoal-colored hair intertwines in his magnificent breastplate of pipe-bone tied at his neck and waist. The moccasins on his feet are beautifully beaded but threadbare. The other sits saddled, weathered and worn, a hand-rolled cigarette dangling from the corner of his mouth. Strapped at his waist are heavy chaparajos protecting his legs. His hat sits low on his head, blocking the mighty rays of the sun.
>
> The lonesome howl of a coyote, echoing in the canyon, distracts the two acquaintances. They pull their horses away . . . suddenly, the enticing sound of the coyote becomes an annoying whimper of the domesticated dog wanting to go for his early-morning walk. The transition from this fantasy to reality is common for this woman. She always dreams of the Wild West. It is an escape from a hectic, materialistic, and often *faux* society, to what she perceives as a more peaceful, naturalistic and always meaningful world.
>
> Many aspects of her life are somehow influenced by this era. It began when she was a little girl riding her rocking horse for hours. Later, as a teenager, her mother, who was raised in New Mexico, gave her some turquoise earrings that had belonged to a *real* Indian princess. Nevertheless, this love for the West has become more profound over the years, so much so that she almost accepted a teaching position on a Navaho Indian Reservation in New Mexico. However, a marriage proposal conflicted with her plans and she never made it to the reservation. Instead, she has captured the spirit of the West in her home.

Reflections

In my 1988 dissertation, a study of children as writers, I defined authorship as

> the processes a writer engages in while expressing uniqueness in ideas and experiences through written language in a manner representing personal feelings, expression, and style. In addition, it describes the connection between writer and text, whereby the writer invests oneself throughout the composing process, resulting in a sense of ownership in the finished product.

When teachers who were involved in this writing workshop wrote about their writing processes, they revealed a heightened awareness of authorship as I defined it. For example, the author of the previous excerpt noted:

> I believe this was one of the most difficult papers I have written since the 7th grade! When I was thinking about why it was so hard for me to write, I came to the conclusion that it was because I had so much freedom as to the topic and style of the paper. I am not used to this! I cannot remember another time in high school or college that I have been given such free rein over my writing. I must say that, in the end, it was a most satisfying experience.

Others shared similar feelings, as demonstrated in the following excerpt written by a second-grade teacher:

> This was the hardest paper I think I've ever had to write. I just finished it, and I feel exhausted. I'm emotionally and physically drained. It takes so much energy and strength to write from your heart. This kind of writing is hard work.

Witnessing the development of this sense of authorship in my students has left me hopeful that these teachers will make some effort to transfer what they learned in our workshop to their own classrooms. To that end, the following sample of their written comments is most encouraging:

> Although I have worked extremely hard, this assignment has been a rewarding experience for me. I am happy with the progress of my writing. It has made me aware that I need a lot of time to think and reflect before I write. I don't do well in a hurried situation, but this is all right. We all have different process needs to produce our best work. As I enter a new school year, I want to provide a writing climate that will encourage

and allow for differences in process styles so that each author can create to his/her maximum ability.

(Fifth-grade teacher)

This was one of the hardest assignments I have ever had but it really made me stop and think about myself and how I do write. I know that now and forever I am a writer. I will forever remember this assignment especially when I ask my students to write. I never knew the writing process could take so long and involve so much thought. From now on I will be considerate of the author's time and allow them the freedom to write about topics that cause their creative juices to flow.

(First-grade teacher)

Although I cannot locate the source, Donald Graves has been quoted as saying:

When writing, Americans too often feel like the man who has been invited to a party of distinguished guests. Being a person of modest station, he attends with great reluctance and discomfort. He has limited aims: to be properly attired, demonstrate correct manners, say as little as possible and leave early.

Unlike Graves's "partygoers," I am encouraged that the teachers in my class were willing to put aside their misgivings about writing long enough to get caught up in the spirit of authorship. By doing so, they were able to participate fully in the writing "parties" celebrated in our classroom. I believe that their participation in the "Writing Experience Project" had much to do with this.

Work Cited

Nistler, Robert J. 1988. "A Descriptive Analysis of Good Readers' and Writers' Concepts of Authorship at Grades One, Three, and Five." Ph.D. diss. University of Texas at Austin. *DAI* (1989) 50-02A, p. 348.

5 Writing a Student Profile

Lela M. DeToye
Southern Illinois University at Edwardsville

When asked to recall their early literacy development, most education majors I encounter have either forgotten or romanticized those experiences. What were their favorite books as first graders? How did they feel when asked to read aloud in front of a classroom of peers? How did they deal with unknown words when they were first learning to read? The real answers have usually been lost with the passage of time.

However, the answers to such questions are crucial to students who are preparing to become teachers. Recalling these experiences can help them develop empathy with their students as well as focus their own teaching strategies. Yet college students' personal responses to these questions may not only be clouded by time and distance, but also be biased in that they, as successful college students and preparing teachers, consider themselves the success stories of education. They "recall" having had positive enough experiences in elementary school, so they want to return there to teach.

As a professor of language arts methods classes, I try to put my students in touch with the realities of early literacy development—not just the success stories, but also the everyday stories and the less than happy ones. To do that, my students need access to elementary students, preferably of primary school age. At my university, each elementary methods class is tied to a half day of field experience in an elementary school.

Access to a classroom of students, however, is not enough. To get the real and honest stories of early literacy development, a one-on-one closeness between college student and primary student is necessary. Therefore, very early each semester, my students, in consultation with their cooperating teachers, select one student from their field placement classroom to interview. Through a series of interviews that focus on the child's early literacy development, my college students experience all over again what it is like to learn to read and write in a public setting.

Some of the questions for these interviews are prompted by the personal relationship between the college student and the primary student. Many, however, are the result of lectures, readings, and discussions in the methods class. Over several semesters, we have generated a list of open-ended questions that have been relatively successful in getting primary students to offer thoughtful responses.

Interview Questions

1. What does it mean to be a good listener? How can you tell when someone is listening to you?

2. When and how did you learn to read? Who first tried to teach you?

3. Tell me a funny story about when you were learning to talk. What were the first words you said? What did they sound like?

4. What was the first book you remember reading or having read to you? When and where do you like to read or be read to?

5. What kinds of books do you like to read now? Who is your favorite author? Why? Your favorite illustrator? Why?

6. What do you like or dislike about writing your own stories? What kinds of stories do you like to write?

7. How do you decide which books to pick from the library?

8. How do you feel when you have to speak or read in front of the class?

9. Why is it important to learn to read? Write?

10. When you are reading, what do you do when you come to a word you don't know?

11. When you are writing, what do you do when you want to use a word you don't know how to spell?

These interviews are tape-recorded. Segments of them are shared in peer groups in the methods class. The students discuss the variety and richness of the responses, and compare them with their own recollections of early literacy experiences and with the theory and research we are reading and discussing.

From Interview to Student Profile

The story of these interviews, however, does not end with this rich and valuable discussion. As the language arts methods professor, I want my students to learn about and to value process writing; as the director of a National Writing Project site, I know that the best way to accom-

---

Student Profile Assignment

In the voice of a primary school student, write an introduction about yourself as a language user. Begin with your memories about early literacy experiences and then bring us up to date on how you currently feel about and engage in reading, writing, speaking, and listening. Aim your introduction at a group of preparing teachers who are interested in how you developed as a language user.

To The Writer:

Purpose: To introduce your primary student to your language arts methods class. We want to be able to "see" that student as a developing language user.

Audience: Fellow preparing teachers interested in literacy development.

Voice: The primary age student whom you interviewed.
Suggestion: To maintain the voice of the child, use your tape recording to capture his/her exact words and sentence structures.

Figure 1. Student profile assignment.

plish this is by becoming a writer oneself. Thus, these tape-recorded interviews and the resulting discussion become the prewriting for a student profile that my college students develop through the steps of the writing process.

The assignment for this profile appears in figure 1. Using these guidelines, each student prepares a rough draft of the student profile. These initial drafts are shared in peer groups. The discussion focuses on each writer's effectiveness in maintaining the voice of the primary student while revealing that student as a developing language user. Based on this discussion, the rough draft is revised, and a second draft is brought back to the same peer group. This time the discussion focuses on the effectiveness of the revisions, and suggestions are made for cleaning up the surface errors that remain in the paper.

This cleanup procedure always brings up questions about spelling and appropriate grammar. If the paper is supposed to exhibit the voice of a primary student, some liberties with conventional usage and structure must be allowed. As the students struggle to capture this voice on paper, we have authentic opportunities to discuss the developmental nature of a child's growth in the area of usage and spelling. My students can see and hear the logic behind many of the usage "mistakes" their placement students are making. By listening to the speech of their students, they understand why they spell the way they do. This activity also helps my college students understand that purpose and voice are controlling factors in the amount and kinds of editing that should be done on any writing assignment.

Throughout this extended assignment, my students and I have many opportunities to study and discuss a wide range of language arts concerns: language acquisition and development, the connection between reading and writing development in the primary grades, inventive grammar and spelling, the writing process, the importance of student attitudes in the development of reading and writing, and many others. Going through the writing process as writers causes them to empathize with their placement students and to think about the expectations for writing that they placed on them. My students understand, firsthand, the constraints that students feel while writing and in sharing their writing with peers and teachers. They then apply this knowledge in the language arts lessons that they plan for their placement students.

To complete the description of this language arts methods activity, I offer the following excerpt from a finished student profile:

> When I was five, I realized that reading was fun. I'm always looking for something funny to read. I like to write stories that make people laugh, too. I can remember my parents first reading to me when I was about two. They were funny stories, too. Now I read to my parents, and they listen.
>
> In the first grade, I remember reading a really funny story about a boy and a girl who were learning how to skate. I read how they tied pillows to their bottoms so they wouldn't fall down the stairs on their skates. They fell down anyway and made a big BOOM!
>
> Now I'm in the third grade, and we read long stories. We are doing "Book-It" for pizza at school, and we get extra points for reading long stories. Some of us even read when my teacher is giving us directions. We just go straight to our desk and read! When I'm in class and come to a word that I don't know, I skip it and let the rest of the sentence give me a clue about the word. If that doesn't work, I look at the word and especially the vowels. Every word has a vowel, you know. Next, I look at the consonants and sound it out. Then I know the word.

6 Teachers as Writers

D. R. Ransdell
University of Arizona

In *A Rhetoric for Writing Teachers*, Erika Lindemann (1982) explains that students deem rewriting unimportant because "their teachers neglect it, rarely demonstrating *how* rewriting works" (182). I have to agree. As an undergraduate, I took five creative writing workshops. Although all my professors were published authors, and each of them mentioned the need to rewrite, none ever explained how to go about it, much less actually showed revision in action. When I first taught composition, I was prompted to bring in drafts of my own writing after students accused me of not remembering how hard it was to write. I wanted to convince them that most writers need to work hard to revise their work, and that my suggestion that they write several drafts of their essays was a reasonable one.

Rewriting has always been an important part of my writing. Even as an undergraduate, I was rarely satisfied with the draft I wrote on the first try. I wasn't discouraged by this; I knew about Hemingway and all the endings of *A Farewell to Arms*. When drawing up the first assignment sheet for my college students, I automatically divided the project into broad stages the students might strive for: first draft—overview and general organization; second draft—organization and information within paragraphs; third draft—style and grammar. I wanted to encourage my students to rethink their drafts, making extensive changes if necessary, as well as to carefully edit their writing as they approached a finished product. (For a more explicit and reasoned account of rewriting, see Lindemann's "Teaching Rewriting," chapter 12 in *A Rhetoric for Writing Teachers*.) When I went over the assignment sheet in class, I met with resistance.

"This is a joke, right?" asked Dave. Dave sat in the front row. After two weeks of class, he was already my least favorite student because he was always the most ready to complain.

Many thanks to Greg Glau for helpful comments on this essay—D.R.R.

"These are guidelines. Maybe you don't need to write many drafts," I replied.

"But you're not going to grade us by how many drafts we do, or are you?"

"If you can get everything right the first time, that's great. Most writers find it easier to improve their work by writing several drafts, concentrating on different aspects of their writing at different times."

"Yeah, but when you write, you don't do this, do you?" asked Louise. Louise was always trying to get out of work, but at least she was friendly about it. "You probably don't have to write at all," she ventured.

Several students nodded in agreement. It was a challenge I couldn't resist: "I had a magazine article come out last spring. If anybody's interested, I can bring it in and explain the steps I went through to write it." To my surprise, everyone seemed interested.

At home, I had five successive versions of "Traveling with the Experts" on disk, and I spent a few minutes studying the changes. As usual, I had added and deleted, rearranged the structure, modified the tone, eased out awkward phrases, and slaved over single word choices. "Some pieces of writing come easily, without a great deal of internal revision," says Donald Murray (1978). "The experience is rare for most writers, however, and it usually comes after a lifetime of discipline" (92). I was still about a lifetime behind.

My biggest battle had been with the introduction. While parts of my draft remained constant from one version to the next, each opening was different. I decided it would be helpful to show my students different versions of the introduction so that we could talk about concrete changes. I chose the three most diverse opening paragraphs and printed them out on the same page for easy comparison. I also printed out a complete version of each draft, which I intended to pass around in class so that my students could get an idea of the extent of my revisions.

The next day, I began the period by asking students about their own experiences with writing and about what gave them difficulty. They agreed that getting started was the hardest part, and I confessed that the same was true for me. As I handed out the sheet with introductions, I explained that I had gone to Greece on our university's study tour and that the article I had written was for *Transitions Abroad*, an educational travel magazine. The students seemed to enjoy the fact that I was sharing an outside interest with them. Most had heard about the university tour, but they were surprised that I had been a recent participant. They were even more surprised that I had three versions of the same short introduction. I asked them to read all three:

[First Draft]

Nearly everyone has seen pictures of the Parthenon. If you go to Athens and have the chance to see it firsthand, that's even better, but unless you know a lot about archaeology, you won't know much about what you're seeing, no matter how many times you read the guidebook. One solution is to go to Greece with a university group. That way you get the best possible information, and you'll understand exactly what you're seeing.

[Second Draft]

If you ever go to Athens, no doubt you'll visit the Parthenon. The problem is that you won't know what you're seeing. Any guidebook will give you an explanation, but who's ever heard of a "peristyle" or a "stylobate"? If you really want to find out about the Parthenon, one solution is to join up with a university program, and tour Greece with them. It's a more expensive way to travel, but it's also worth the money.

[Third Draft]

Any trip to Athens will naturally include the Parthenon, and any guidebook will give you information about it. The problem is that unless you're a trained archaeologist, you might not be able to decipher what the guidebook says. If you really want to find out about the Parthenon, one solution is to join a university study tour. Not only can you collect credit in the humanities, but you can also get top explanations about all the sites on your itinerary.

As we looked at some of the concrete aspects of the drafts, I asked the students to outguess me by offering explanations for specific changes. They were perceptive editors. They easily reasoned that I had changed from "Nearly everyone has seen pictures of the Parthenon" to "If you ever go to Athens . . . " in order to target more closely my actual subject: traveling in Greece. They agreed that the second sentence of my first version was simply too long; in fact, they delighted in pointing out that I had four commas in a single sentence, since I had once commented that multiple commas can be a sign for revision.

When I gave them a slight hint, they also surmised that I switched "The problem is that you *won't* know what you're seeing" to "might," to avoid offending the audience, and they positively enjoyed the "tour/them" object error at the end of the second draft. In general, they decided that the last attempt was the most successful, but some maintained that I should have kept the question "Who's ever heard of a 'peristyle' or a 'stylobate'?" in the final version. Suddenly, I had defenders on both sides arguing about the effectiveness of my writing.

"I like the question because it breaks things up," said one student.

"It's a bad sentence because it sounds like the writer is trying to be too sophisticated by throwing words around," replied another.

"The question makes the writing more interesting because you have to think of an answer," commented a third.

It was flattering to have my students debating a moot point.

"But it's not really wrong either way?" asked Louise.

"It has to do with style," I told her. "If the question makes the introduction less appealing to you, then it's wrong. If it makes the introduction more interesting, then it's all right. In fact, I took that question in and out about five times. If I had done the final version on another day, when I was in a different mood, maybe I would have left it in."

My students were intrigued by the fact that I could not give them an absolute answer. In the meantime, I handed out copies of the printed article and passed around the drafts. I also talked about some of the larger organizational changes.

Dave had the drafts at his desk and was looking through them, page by page. "You had to do all this work for only one short article? This is like a nightmare." For a brief moment, even Dave was endearing. If nothing else, I figured he might finish the semester with a greater appreciation for written material. "It's not that bad. It just takes patience," I replied.

The students asked more questions about my writing, but no one stopped to talk to me after class. For a while, I was afraid I might have inhibited their writing by making the prospect of completing an essay more daunting than before; now, they had a better idea of the amount of work I expected. When I collected the papers for their first essays, I was pleased to see bold, roughly penned codes such as "Rough Draft #1" and "Another Draft" along with their completed essays. By studying their different versions, I noticed that many had reworked the structure of their pieces, and virtually everyone had written several trial introductions.

While I found a lot of weak areas in their writing, I was also pleased that most were past what Sommers (1980) refers to as the "thesaurus" approach to rewriting (381) so early in the semester. Several of the students were still disappointed when their multiple drafts did not receive the high grades they were hoping for, but when I offered them the opportunity to submit another draft, they did. During the course of the semester, the average number of drafts my students submitted increased, and so did the quality of their writing. Even though they occasionally grew tired of working on drafts of the same paper, none questioned the benefits of revision.

Since teaching that first composition class, I have shown each new class the process I go through for my own work. I might not be able to turn all my students into writers, but I can encourage them to broaden their perspectives on how to write and how to improve their writing. Most of all, I can show them that writing presents a challenge to all writers, not just student writers, and that good writing is more often achieved by the painstaking work of rewriting than by the lucky moment when inspiration hits and everything comes out right the first time.

Works Cited

Lindemann, Erika. 1982. *A Rhetoric for Writing Teachers.* New York: Oxford University Press.

Murray, Donald. 1978. "Internal Revision: A Process of Discovery." In *Research on Composing: Points of Departure,* edited by Charles R. Cooper and Lee Odell, 85–103. Urbana: NCTE.

Sommers, Nancy. 1980. "Revision Strategies of Student Writers and Experienced Adult Writers." *College Composition and Communication* 31: 378–88.

7 Group Paragraphs: A Route to Revision

Elaine Murphy
Ursuline Academy, Dallas, Texas

Despite some teachers' glowing success with peer editing, I have, for some reason, always encountered student resistance. Perhaps it's because students often believe that editing implies simply circling mechanical errors and that a critique means finding fault. While more capable writers do exhibit some understanding that true revision involves overhauling and then fine-tuning a paper, few students, initially, have the courage to point out to a peer that her paper, quite frankly, still needs much work. And from a practical standpoint, many peer editors simply think they have no stake in another student's paper and often spend class editing time glancing across the table at their own papers, nervously anticipating the "atrocities" that a peer may be performing on their work.

Admittedly, successful peer editing takes time: time to develop an understanding of the purposes of editing and revision, and time to foster trust and honesty among students. But since patience has never been my strong suit, I have turned to group papers as a means for obtaining quicker results.

When I announce that the first writing assignment of the year will be a single, multiparagraph essay produced by three to five students, the reaction is a sigh of relief; the students quickly compute that having five workers will mean one-fifth the work for each one. And, after summer vacation, the students are ripe for an experience featuring group interaction.

On the first day, the small groups work to find an argumentative angle for a limited discussion of the novel that we have just read. Because each student will eventually write a body paragraph in support of the thesis, the group must immediately define terms, clarify the purpose of the entire essay, and organize major ideas. The group technique precludes redundancy; no one wants the body paragraph she will write at home tonight to overlap the discussion of another student. Fuzzy thinking is also less likely when group members have spent this first fifty-minute period brainstorming and arguing every angle until they have reached consensus. In cases where heated discussion has produced sharpened polarities rather than consensus, the students see the need to write a thesis that reflects the double-edged nature of their arguments. The important point is that students see that any good thesis is the result of a dynamic process of examining all the dimensions of a topic at the outset.

As they write their individual body paragraphs at home, the students are conscious of their responsibility to the group: Does my paragraph represent the ideas we brainstormed in class today? Is my writing clear enough for the group to understand? Will my paragraph follow logically from the one that will precede it? Am I likely to overlap what Kristen is going to say? Will my examples contradict the point Marla is planning to make in paragraph four?

Sometimes the students return to class the next day frustrated that they have not been able to defend the thesis the group had already agreed upon. Nonetheless, I am elated that they have recognized the dynamism of the writing process. Rough theses usually do need further qualification, I assure them. So on this second day of the project, the students work to adapt the thesis to their new insights on the topic. Those groups needing to undertake massive revision of major concepts at least have the consolation of moral support. I have found my students less willing to undertake this kind of questioning and revision in an essay written entirely on their own and later submitted for peer critique. Here, however, there is simply no room for complacency when everyone has a stake in the whole project.

Usually on the third day, the group is ready to piece together the paragraphs into a cohesive essay. However, even after revising transitions and topic sentences, even after rearranging and deleting to guarantee continuity and flow, the paragraphs, inexplicably, seem just a little off balance. Again, some students will experience frustration in achieving a somewhat disjointed effect, despite painstaking efforts to apply all the revision techniques in their writing repertoires. To others comes an amazing revelation: We actually have our own writing styles, and part of the disequilibrium we are now experiencing comes from that fact!

Although they work to even out the differences by agreeing to adopt a certain level of diction and similar tone, many students persist in seeing the stylistic individuality of the body paragraphs as a problem. And while this unevenness would be an obvious problem in an essay produced by a single student, this spontaneously drawn, practical lesson on the definition of style, which the group paper drives home so dramatically, is, to me, worth the admitted drawback. Of course, some of the less capable writers will be disturbed that their paragraphs are stylistically less effective than those of the others. Most freely admit, however, that what they have already produced is superior—because of the group brainstorming and discussion of revision techniques—to what they would have written in an individual essay. And the more capable writers, although they will not be directly graded on the body paragraph of another student, seem more willing, than in most traditional peer-revision conferences, to become actively involved in making suggestions.

After rewriting individual body paragraphs on the third night, most groups will spend the fourth day collaborating on an introductory paragraph that will do justice to the entire essay. Each writer has a stake in ensuring that the introduction provides a proper lead-in to the ideas of her body paragraph. Also, because the group experience has already made the students keenly aware that they write for others, they generally have no problem in keeping an even broader readership in mind as they write the introduction. Consequently, ways to evoke reader interest and to ensure understanding become the focus of the day.

Writing a concluding paragraph becomes a kind of retrospective of the group experience. Because we want the conclusion to be more than just a repetition of the parts of the body, groups begin the task by retracing the thought processes of the past week: How did we begin? Where did we arrive? Why did our final thesis prove more valid than our original one? What of any real importance did we learn? In this way, the conclusion not only becomes more analytical than summative, but students take time to assess the value of their collective efforts.

On the final day, the groups read the completed essay for continuity and, finally, engage in the task that most of them had originally considered the sum total of revision: mechanical correction. Having spent so much of the week dealing with major changes, the students can now take these nitty-gritty revisions in stride. Each student makes a final draft of her body paragraph while two volunteers offer to transcribe the agreed-upon versions of the introduction and conclusion.

Although the project probably can operate within any teacher's grading system, my students have found it most equitable to receive an individual grade for their own body paragraph and group grades for brainstorming notes (prewriting, outline, etc.), the introduction, the conclusion, and the effectiveness of the essay as an organic whole. The students who piloted the project several years ago also asked to include their personal evaluations of each member's contributions. I feared a gripe session about who tried to freeload and who bogged down the project, but I was pleasantly surprised when this kind of negativism never materialized. Instead, they wanted me to know, for example, that although Sam did help Katie revise her body paragraph, it was Katie who provided the impetus for the first day of brainstorming. All the notes, as well as the final draft, were in Susan's script not only because she has the best handwriting, but because she always listens well and takes the most meticulous notes. One group was even astute enough to note that one member would always provide interesting, though sometimes oblique, general observations, for which another member was able to provide substantiation and a more specific focus.

Since this generous and farsighted group first presented the notion, I have introduced the project to subsequent classes by emphasizing that each member's peculiar strengths would surely enhance the entire project, and therefore, no member's contribution could be downgraded. The informal evaluation suggested by that first class has now become an important vehicle for building class unity and acknowledging each member's worth. On a more pragmatic level, it has also reduced the natural human tendency to allow—or to force—the strongest writer in the group to do all the composing, since we stress that writing involves a number of skills. If a student should show a lack of willingness to participate, and if peer encouragement does not resolve the problem, I might intervene only to suggest that the student be assigned the role which best utilizes her strengths. Flattery seems preferable to coercion.

In those few cases where students remain recalcitrant, they discover in future joint projects that others are hesitant to take them in. "This setup is like real life," one student responded to an anonymous postproject evaluation. "Some people are lazy or can't be trusted. They really have to work hard in a second project to regain their place in the group," stated another. "I didn't feel well during the project, and so I guess I didn't give my best. My group was pretty understanding, but I still feel I have to make it up to them in the second paper," replied a third. The group project also enhances attendance, as absentees face the prospect of completing the project alone and risk the disapproval of a group they have disappointed.

Another gratifying by-product has been an increased comfort level in large-group discussions. Because the students have argued so freely in their small groups and found affirmation without teacher intervention, they have a keener sense of class discussion as dialogue rather than a question-and-answer forum. "Some people get violent about insisting on their ideas in the group," offered one student. "Still, I surprised myself that I cared enough about my ideas to fight back."

When I write, I favor a quiet retreat where I can leisurely roll ideas around in my head or scribble furiously as the mood moves me. And while I certainly provide my students with many opportunities to do the same, the students' need for peer involvement and immediate feedback makes the group paper a viable alternative to traditional writing experiences.

8 Glossing: A Revision Technique

Marylyn E. Calabrese
Malvern, Pennsylvania

One of the challenges writing teachers face is handling the paper load when students revise. The task of evaluating the revised draft and comparing it with the original is a juggling process that is both demanding and time-consuming. Teachers often find it necessary to reread the original draft, skimming their suggestions for revision, and then to read the new draft, switching back and forth as needed. Sometimes the task is so daunting that responding to a totally different draft seems preferable, and for that reason alone, some teachers hesitate to require revisions.

"Glossing" (the process of writing explanatory notes in the margin of a text) is a simple technique that students can use to identify where and how the revised draft is different from the original. Students make brief annotations (the "gloss") on the revised text, explaining each change they have made. With the original draft (along with readers' comments) attached to a revised, "glossed" draft, a teacher can now evaluate a student's revision quickly and easily. Additionally, glossing teaches students that revising is not haphazard guesswork, but a process *they* control.

How It Started

Glossing was born of necessity. Several years ago, when word-processed papers first became commonplace in my classroom, it wasn't long before students discovered a shortcut to revision: put a new date on an old draft, make a clean printout, and maybe the reader will not notice that few revisions have been made. After becoming frustrated and annoyed with trying to find exactly where the revised paper differed from the original, I started asking students to identify all revised passages and explain what they had done.

Although my original purpose was to expedite my responses to their papers, I soon discovered that the technique had a salutary effect on my students. Because they now had to identify and explain their revisions, they began to take them more seriously. Whereas before they might have rewritten an opening paragraph hurriedly, hoping it would somehow pass muster, they were now more careful because they had to explain what they had done. Most heartening was that, as students used these annotations, their revised papers began to show real improvement.

Now, I use glossing not only with all word-processed revisions, but with handwritten ones as well. In fact, I do not accept a major revision without the proper annotations, and, of course, not without the original draft for comparison. In oral conferences, I always ask each student to explain how the new draft differs from the previous one.

What the Student Does

Glossing works best with papers that do not need a total rewrite. A revision that has either a new topic or an entirely new perspective on the original topic would not be suitable. For just about all other papers, however, glossing can easily be used to note corrections of mechanical errors, changes in sentence structure, and revisions of unclear passages, missing examples, wordiness, etc.

How does glossing work? A student writer begins with the draft of a paper, one that has been commented on and is going to be revised. Noting all readers' suggestions—comments from peers and the teacher—she prepares a revised draft. On the revised copy, the student marks all changes. Although these markings can be underlining or brackets, I prefer colored highlighting, because it is easier to see and because the students seem to enjoy making their usual black-and-white typed copies more colorful. (One of my more creative students even uses different colors to denote different kinds of changes: blue highlighting is mechanics, red passages have changes in meaning, etc. Although her revisions often look like rainbows, they are very easy to read.)

Then, in the margins of any highlighted section, line, or word (it might be a single mark of punctuation), the student writes a word or brief comment (whatever is needed) to explain the change and the reason it was made. Here are some of the annotations my students use frequently:

sp	corrected punctuation
syn	varied sentence structure
quoted less	explained examples
changed title	new concluding paragraph
gave more analysis	added examples as requested

omitted words for clarity	linked more closely to thesis
tightened sentence structure	stronger opening sentence
moved sentence to front of paragraph to highlight thesis	rewrote thesis to better reflect paper's content

Although these annotations take only a few minutes of the students' time to write, they help the students take more responsibility for their revisions. Now, when they write, "I changed the opening to make it clearer," they begin to articulate—to themselves—their own writing process.

What the Teacher Does

In responding to a revised paper, one of the key tasks is to identify changes from the original draft. Must I reread the original paper, then skim the readers' suggestions before tackling the new draft? This is where the real value of glossing comes in for the teacher. Now it is possible to look at the new draft, note the changes—which have been bracketed and glossed—check back to the original, see what the suggestions were, and note whether sufficient improvements have been made. Is the opening paragraph stronger? Are the transitional sentences tighter? Have the mechanical errors been corrected?

Now the teacher can easily find and focus on the revised passages, rather than taking the time to reread everything. Naturally, if the revision is totally different from the original, a thorough reading is warranted. Even then I ask students to explain why they started over and exactly what they did.

Figure 1 shows both the student's gloss and the teacher's responses. I have included the opening of an essay that a student prepared for her college application. The topic was "My Family."

Benefits for Teacher and Student

When students gloss their revisions, the teacher's reading time is greatly reduced. Responding to a set of revised and glossed papers (approximately twenty-five two-page papers) with the originals attached can take less than an hour.

But the value to the students is even greater. Although some of their annotations are mundane and superficial, many reflect a growing understanding of what revision really means. I find that as students articulate their writing process, they begin to take those necessary steps toward mastery and control. It is all part of the process of ownership. When they have to tell others how and why they changed their writing, they seem to get closer to saying, "This is mine."

First draft with teacher's comments

Great start but incomplete. Keep going.

nice opening sentence. Whenever I describe my family to my friends,

Link needed

they think I'm part of the Mafia. One of the

I want to know more.

most important assets when growing up. My *Sent str?*

family is a modified joint family that has

become very close through business relations.

Sounds interesting. Please expand. How is your family important to you?

Revised draft with student's gloss

Whenever I describe my family to my friends,

Link provided

they think I'm part of the Mafia. [I'm really

not part of the Mafia, but I do have connec-

Expanded and developed more.

tions all around the world through business

relations. Through starting a business

empire, giving me an opportunity to explore

the world and allowing me to be a part of

Explained how family is important.

their crusade to end poverty, my family has

greatly influenced me in determining the

type of person I am.]

Figure 1. Draft and revision showing teacher's commentary and student's glosses. (The bracketed portion shows the revisions.)

II Exploiting the Portfolio

New ideas in the teaching of English do come along. Some of them become quickly established in practice because they are so right, so timely, so useful. The portfolio in writing classes is a case in point.

Writing portfolios typically contain a selection from the student's total writing output over a given time, a selection chosen by the student to represent his or her overall performance. Usually, the selected pieces have been revised and polished.

The portfolio approach was first designed as a way to evaluate students' work, as an alternative to the separate marking of every final draft, and has since been extended to teacher and program evaluations. But portfolios have also become important teaching tools in many classrooms, being used to honor writing, to motivate revision, to build self-esteem, and to develop student sensitivity about what makes for good writing.

In this section, practicing teachers report candidly on their experiences with this teaching/assessing practice. Joseph E. Strzepek and Margo A. Figgins open with "A Polemic on Evaluating Writing," in which they highlight the negative effects of certain traditional beliefs about writing evaluation. They go on to show how a more progressive evaluation system can work and how the portfolio fits into that system.

Carole Ackerson Bertisch, in "The Portfolio as an Assessment Tool," makes the important point that portfolios can lead to responsible, productive student choice. She cites a pattern of increasing sophistication in a portfolio program, showing students heavily engaged in metacognition about their own growth as writers.

A group of Northern Virginia Writing Project colleagues (including Strzepek and Figgins) offers us a wide-ranging series of experiential commentaries on the use of portfolios at the secondary school and college levels. In "The Empty Space," Linda LaMantia Privette draws on a ballet rehearsal metaphor to show the portfolio under development, generating productive dialogue and positive student response.

Bob Ingalls presents "Interviewing a Portfolio," where he makes discoveries about the writers as persons, the writers at work, the products and value of writing.

In "Teenage Mutant Ninja Portfolios," Dan Verner confesses his struggle to make portfolios work, a struggle with a happy ending, he reports. Much of the turmoil here was in seeking to balance process and product.

In "Portfolios: From Negative to Positive," Anne Sharp reports in an anecdotal way about how she got into portfolios via the principal's office door and how she made something genuinely instructive for her students out of the experience.

Another personal journey to portfolio use is chronicled by Donald R. Gallehr in "Portfolio Assessment in the College Writing Classroom." This journey starts with the professor's annual performance evaluation and ends in a circle in the composition classroom.

In "What Student Portfolios Are Teaching Us," Laura Brady and Christopher Thaiss describe how a program to exempt college seniors from a composition class led to some significant discoveries about the value of portfolios and of the writing process essays they had required as part of those portfolios.

9 A Polemic on Evaluating Writing

Joseph E. Strzepek
University of Virginia

Margo A. Figgins
University of Virginia

Why do so many language arts teachers, from the upper elementary grades through high school, persist in using grading practices that constrain their teaching repertoires and muzzle their students' growth as writers? Despite breakthroughs in knowledge about how students acquire writing skills, how both students and professionals actually write, and how teachers have successfully empowered even first-grade writers, a stubborn majority resists the testaments of James Moffett, Peter Elbow, Donald Murray, and Donald Graves, and their successors, Lucy Calkins and Nancie Atwell. This intransigent majority continues to resist the legions of apostles sent forth from the National Writing Project's numerous sites.

Resistance to alternative grading practices manifests itself in the custom of grading every discrete writing assignment, and in teachers' authoritarian control of their students' choices of subject and genre. In this essay, we will examine the beliefs that underlie these traditional practices. We will also identify beliefs and practices that empower student writers to define their own genres and topics and to evaluate their own writing as it moves through the writing process and accumulates in an evolving portfolio of finished works and works in progress. We will suggest how teachers can join the progressive movement of those who document their students' growth in writing not with percentages or letter grades in an impersonal ledger, but by the more vital evidence contained in the students' portfolios. Consider, first, what some teachers we interviewed have told us, directly or indirectly, about how they grade writing and why they grade that way:

Traditional Beliefs about Grading Writing

1. If I assign a piece of writing, *I* must grade it or the students will not take it seriously. They might not even do it. I do not trust them to give each other or themselves appropriate evalu-

ation, because they do not have the experience or training. *I am the paid expert.*

2. I evaluate student writing the way a doctor gives a physical: privately, confidentially, professionally. Students should accept my diagnoses and follow my prescriptions. They should not compare notes with others or seek second opinions.

3. In order to grade fairly, I must have time to mark errors and write comments to explain a paper's grade. So, I limit the length and quantity of papers I assign, and I restrict the topics and genres to those in which I am expert myself.

4. I maintain my authority by acting as an evaluator, not as a writer. How I write is my business. My job is to identify the literate and the illiterate. Not everyone can learn to write well.

5. I follow the dictates of my department and school, even if their notions of evaluation do not reflect the best professional practices. Their authority supersedes mine.

6. Change is not possible. By the time students enter my class, the grading die has been cast. If I were to alter my evaluation methods, my students would be confused. I would also antagonize their future teachers, should my students learn to expect a more student-centered evaluation.

7. Because students are in competition for grades—and should be—to prepare for college and life, I strictly limit collaboration in composing, revising, and editing to prevent friends from plagiarizing and enemies from cruelly attacking each other's work. I also discourage the use of word processors and spell checkers, because not all students can afford them, and because those machines mask incompetencies in handwriting and spelling.

8. Since writing poetry, fiction, and drama depends on creativity and imagination, not all students can be required to write in those genres. Nor can such writing be objectively graded. I will only assign it as a bonus option. We should, however, allow creative writing in elective classes for our latent poets and novelists, provided their parents consent.

Consider the negative effects of these beliefs and practices: The teacher, not the student, owns the writing—from the topic, to the mode and the length, all the way to the grade. Grading criteria stress form and mechanics over authenticity and originality in voice, language, and perception. Teachers spend most of their time evaluating student writing products, instead of guiding students through whatever writing processes are appropriate to their purposes.

Listing these traditional beliefs and their negative effects is not an exercise in hyperbole. Each belief has been asserted during observations and interviews with conscientious teachers. The major effect of these beliefs is that they limit a writing teacher's repertoire to what George Hillocks calls the "presentational mode." According to Hillocks, in *Research on Written Composition* (1986), his metanalysis of hundreds of empirical studies, the teacher-centered presentational approach is considerably less effective in improving student writing than either the "natural process mode" or the "environmental mode" (247). The natural process mode permits students to follow their own interests and emphasizes personal writing. The environmental mode stresses the use of guided inquiry and revision strategies on topics or problems in specific academic areas. Both of these modes stress the use of numerous invention, revision, and small-group, workshop feedback strategies.

Many of the teachers we have worked with are painfully aware that traditional grading practices limit implementation of these alternative modes. Although teachers can acknowledge the inhibiting effects of their traditional beliefs and practices, they fear the loss of control inherent in converting to a new set of beliefs and practices. Conversion can be chaotic and frightening, especially if we have no reference point other than a vague dissatisfaction or guilt over our present practices. Letting go of habits, even bad ones, is extremely difficult when teachers have none to replace them.

Fortunately, the National Writing Project and college and university preservice classes are preparing teachers to teach composition by having them perform as writers who can then demonstrate to their students a variety of writing-process strategies. As a result, many teachers are now writing with students and using both the natural process and the environmental modes in teaching writing. Unfortunately, these same teachers often sabotage their greater effectiveness by their compulsion to grade at almost every stage of writing instruction; students are even being *tested on their ability to list and define in appropriate sequence* every step in *the* writing process, from invention through publication! Thus students may come to believe that the "writing process" is a rigid sequence of fixed behaviors rather than understanding it as a fluid, recursive series of options.

We suggest, instead, deferring grading until a substantial portfolio of student writing has accumulated. Then, together *with* their students, teachers can make holistic evaluations of the writing as a body of work, while also noting the relative strengths and weaknesses of individual pieces. Portfolio grading and student self-evaluation require us to adopt a different set of governing assumptions and to reaffirm some uniquely American beliefs—the most important being that almost all students can learn, and therefore should be taught, to write with skill and pride. Whereas extensive writing instruction in European countries is reserved for the elite in business, academia, and politics, American teachers are expected to help all students achieve the writing competencies necessary to succeed in the worlds of work and academia. When those expectations are not met, teachers are severely criticized. Such criticism is unfair when teachers are institutionally restricted from employing teaching and grading practices consistent with democratic expectations. Fortunately, a growing number of teachers and schools are moving in a new direction characterized by a more progressive stance. Listen to what we hear them saying:

Progressive Beliefs and Practices

1. My primary goal is to prepare my students to succeed as learners and citizens in a free society.

2. My grading practices should promote, not subvert, instruction designed to achieve that goal.

3. I provide my students and myself with maximum opportunities for talking, reading, writing, and thinking in a variety of discourse forms, including poetry and fiction. Students and teachers will achieve more growth when they experience themselves as creators and not just consumers of literature.

4. My students can work independently on their own writing projects. As they write for their own purposes, occasions, and audiences, they learn new forms of discourse; they feel an excitement and authority which energizes them and enlightens their peers.

5. Although I withhold grades from specific drafts, I monitor and credit all of my students' attempts at discourse.

6. Students share the responsibility for responding to and monitoring their own and each other's writing. I should not be the only one to evaluate student writing. My students can offer sensitive, helpful responses to each other's work. They often have insights I do not possess.

7. I let my students choose which works they will polish for publication. I consider their accounting of the investment they make in researching and revising specific works when I assess the relative values of the papers in their portfolios.

8. Formative feedback from fellow student writers and me is intrinsic to my whole instructional process. Summative evaluation, grading, is something I do after the fact, holistically, on large portfolios of work in consultation with individual students. Because their work is shared so often in groups, students have a good sense of how their work compares with

that of other students in quantity and quality, and how their performance compares in meeting agreed-upon deadlines. This awareness facilitates agreement between my students and me when we meet to evaluate their portfolios.

9. My students are capable of setting and achieving ambitious and reasonable goals. They can also assess how close they come to meeting them. Assessment that does not include a student's evaluation of his or her own work omits something most significant—the student's personal perception of that work and the degree of ownership realized.

These progressive beliefs and practices are not pipe dreams. Donald Graves, Lucy Calkins, and Nancie Atwell have described in persuasive detail their successes in helping teachers subordinate grading to instruction. But what if a teacher does not have the coaching of a Graves or a Calkins, the stimulation of a Writing Project or Bread Loaf summer institute, or the support of a reasonable principal, as Atwell did? If you are one of the teachers stuck in the rut of continuous, compulsive grading, what might you do?

Ideally, you might find fellow teachers who are, or who would be willing to try, deferring grading until a portfolio of substantial size has accumulated. Together, try to develop firsthand knowledge of how to orchestrate writing instruction and portfolio grading.

Envision your classroom as a studio, not a factory. When you and your students review, in workshop fashion, a paper in progress, listen to the author's assessment of the status of his or her work—rough draft, revision, ready for publication, just needs final editing, best I've ever done, one sorry mess, or whatever. Encourage students to offer their reactions, to describe what they see in the piece so far. Help your students to value their peers' evaluations as well as yours. Make it clear that it is the author's responsibility to choose which papers will be revised and which advice to heed.

Before you submit your grades for any given marking period, have your students submit a self-evaluation form in which they list the strengths and weaknesses of specific papers, identify specific goals for the next marking period, and state what grade they think they deserve for the writing done that marking period. When a student's recommended grade differs from your assessment, meet in conference to reach an understanding, if not complete agreement, on the final grade.

If possible, enroll in a teaching of writing course or writing project that uses as texts Graves's *Writing: Teachers and Children at Work* (1983), Calkins's *Art of Teaching Writing* (1986), and Atwell's *In the Middle* (1987).

Expect your learning process to be a bit bumpy. Both you and your students may take a while to feel comfortable with portfolio grading, but warn your students, your doubting colleagues, principals, and parents: portfolio grading is coming! The Educational Testing Service and the National Writing Project are prompting research studies and training seminars on portfolio assessment. The State of Vermont has instituted a pilot study of portfolio assessment, *Across the Curriculum*, in selected schools. Universities and community colleges, under pressure from legislatures to document growth in student learning, are proposing to show themselves accountable by presenting extensive portfolios of students' work in all subjects, from their freshman through senior years. At the University of Virginia, we are already collecting such work, along with the students' autobiographical assessments of their growth, and we use portfolios to grade students in the classes we teach in the Curry School of Education.

Despite the predominance of traditional beliefs and practices in teaching writing, with patience change is possible. Those of us who use portfolio grading procedures have developed them over years of experience. We continue to adjust our procedures according to our perception of how they best serve our students' growth as writers. We abandoned conventional grading practices because they stifled our best teaching instincts and retarded the progress of all but the most compulsive achievers. We have seen our teaching improve and our students blossom as writers. And we have seen our experiences confirmed again and again in our work with teachers and in the reports of our colleagues at all levels of instruction. Such results return us to our opening question: Given viable alternatives, why do so many teachers continue to employ intrusive and premature grading strategies which have the effect of punishing both students and teachers?

We hope that in this essay, we may have helped teachers and administrators confront their beliefs about grading. We hope this confrontation encourages you to question your current evaluation practices and to give portfolio grading and student self-evaluation a chance. As John Lennon's lyrics might have read: Imagine all our people / writing happily!

Works Cited

Atwell, Nancie. 1987. *In the Middle: Writing, Reading, and Learning with Adolescents.* Upper Montclair, NJ: Boynton/Cook.

Calkins, Lucy M. 1986. *The Art of Teaching Writing.* Portsmouth, NH: Heinemann.

Graves, Donald. 1983. *Writing: Teachers and Children at Work.* Exeter, NH: Heinemann Educational Books.

Hillocks, George, Jr. 1986. *Research on Written Composition: New Directions for Teaching.* Urbana: ERIC/RCS and NCTE.

10 The Portfolio as an Assessment Tool

Carole Ackerson Bertisch
Rye Neck High School, Mamaroneck, New York

After seventeen years of teaching, I am convinced that student choice and participation in assessment are essential elements for successful growth in writing. It is not enough for the teacher to make all the decisions—give assignments, mark errors, return papers with comments and grades. The student must learn and internalize the qualities of good writing. In the past, I found that sometimes I spent more time correcting the paper than the student did writing it. I have since thrown away my red pen and given up scrawled comments in the margin that only I can decipher. Instead, I plan strategies through the use of portfolios which encourage students' growth and responsibility for their own writing. This is not a formula for all teachers, but I hope that my experiences will kindle new ideas for other teachers to help them meet their needs and those of their students.

A Study Initiated

During the past year, I was a member of a portfolio assessment seminar that met at Lehman College as part of the New York City Writing Project. Five high school teachers (three from New York City and two from the suburbs) met with two college teachers and the group leader from the Institute for Literacy Studies. Our purpose was to undertake a searching scrutiny of portfolio assessment.

At the first meeting, when we wrote about our hopes and concerns for this "co-investigation," I wrote, "My methods of evaluation seem skimpy—they need more depth. I feel like a butterfly skimming through the flowers. And I never have enough time."

Since then, my thinking has changed dramatically, and a new method of documentation and evaluation has emerged from our discussions and sharing of ideas. My students have always kept writing folders that contain all of their writing for the year. But the contents of these portfolios, selected from the writing folders, differ because they are papers the students have chosen to revise and edit. The responsibility, therefore, shifts from teacher to student so that by the end of the year, students should be able to evaluate their own strengths and weaknesses and write about them.

My goals for portfolio assessment are as follows:

To encourage student appreciation of good writing—their own and others'.

To have students identify changes in their own work.

To evaluate what is useful to them in class.

To realize that real writers revise and polish and edit.

To review their writing and choose what they think is best.

To understand which pieces of writing lend themselves to revision.

To support each other with positive feedback—to assist, not criticize.

To organize their work for submission.

To estimate their own grades realistically after we establish criteria together.

To allow students to take responsibility for their own writing.

Not all of these goals are new, but each can be incorporated in a new and progressive context.

A New Methodology Instituted

Each class period—now a writing workshop—begins with ten minutes of journal writing, sparked by an idea I place on the board or by some specific need of the students. The students branch off into a range of forms: poetry, letters, personal narratives, fiction, even angry editorials and stream-of-consciousness narratives. Then, for the rest of the workshop session, they may choose to develop mini-lessons or to work with memories, reactions, or visualizations. One student may be polishing a college essay while another is completing a twelve-page mystery. From the beginning, we think about choice and revision. Peer-response groups are active. One student, Stephanie, commenting about the class, observed:

> Writing workshop is a free individual class. We come in ready to write together as a class, but as we do it, [we all have] different thoughts. We might begin with a line from a song to write on, and almost everyone's paper will be an original.

As the year progresses, the portfolios take on different forms. The first portfolios contain the minimum of three polished papers, plus two evaluative pieces. The first piece, an evaluation sheet, is a major step in student self-analysis. It asks the students to list the titles of the submitted papers and to answer the following questions:

1. What changes did you notice in yourself as a writer this quarter?

2. What was the most useful thing you learned about writing this quarter?

3. What grade do you think you deserve? Why?

The second piece consists of students' letters to me about one piece of writing they have chosen to submit; they explain why they chose this particular piece of writing and how it stands out from their other work.

Students find it difficult to adapt to these new matters of choice and participation. Often, they ask me to choose their selections for them. One of the most difficult tasks I have is to refrain from doing so. If I don't, I'll be returning to my old role of critic rather than my new one of coach. But somehow, they do manage to choose. Another student, Jen, commented:

> I selected HEAVEN from the thing we did in class about making a list of all the things we could remember up until first grade. On my list was how I always thought that heaven was on the other side of the bridge near my house. So I decided to write about it. This piece stands out from the rest of my work because it is about something from my past and while I don't remember the details I remembered the main idea and just stemmed off from that.

I respond in writing to each paper they submit in their portfolio and to their letters. Usually, by the time I read these papers, I have heard or read them several times in process, and commented on them individually or as a member of a response group—so the final grading is not very time-consuming for me. Grades given on this portfolio at the end of each quarter are based on effort and improvement as well as the final product.

During the second quarter, students answer two questions about portfolios for my research:

1. If another student asked you what writing workshop is about, how would you describe it? What do you think the goals of the course are?

2. What do you think a portfolio is? What do you think is essential to include in a portfolio during each quarter and at the end of the year? What would represent the important points in your writing?

On the basis of my students' answers, as well as the discussions and readings from my New York City Writing Project seminar, I plan a more complex portfolio for the second quarter. Students fill out the same evaluation sheet but have to write a letter about each of three pieces of writing. Because the letters are used for the midterm grade, in place of an exam, and because the students are beginning to think about the process of writing, their letters usually show evidence of more focused analyses than the letters from the first quarter.

Their midpoint evaluation of their own writing incorporates suggestions from a "Portfolio Reflections" list, subtitled "Thinking about Important Pieces of Your Own Writing." The list contains eight questions taken from Roberta Camp's (1989) article, "Arts Propel: Suggestions for Creating Writing Portfolios." Some of them are reproduced here:

> What do you see as the special strengths of this work?
>
> As a result of your work on this piece, is there a particular technique or interest that you would like to try out or investigate further in future pieces of writing? If so, what is it?
>
> If you could go on working on this piece, what would you do? (Camp 1989, n.p.)

The students are instructed to choose five of the eight questions for each of their three pieces of writing. They write a letter to me for each paper chosen that incorporates their answers. I always find the letters intriguing—the students share thoughts about their writing which I would not discover otherwise, for example:

> When I first wrote this piece, it was in English class around a month and a half ago. I couldn't get past the third paragraph so I put it away with a reminder to myself that I would get back to it really soon. I forgot about it and when I did finally pick it up, it was much easier to write. I had taken a break from it and my head was full of new ideas. So I learned not to throw away pieces of writing that don't seem right or aren't going well because they might sound a lot better after you haven't seen them for a while.

For the third-quarter portfolio, in addition to their three pieces of writing, the students are asked to look through all their writing for the year and describe the changes they observe. They are also asked to write to me about what they hope to accomplish during the fourth, and final, quarter. These questions move them another rung up the ladder of their self-analysis and focus our goals for the remainder of the school year.

For the final, fourth-quarter portfolio, the students are asked to analyze their work in different ways. My goal is to have them think about the types of writing they have done thus far; what they consider their most satisfying piece of writing for the year; what was most useful in class; in what specific ways their writing has changed, based on comments from their third-quarter letters; and their suggestions for future writing workshops. The students complete four response sheets and self-evaluation charts, which are either checkoffs or short answers, rather than formal letters. I schedule an individual conference with each student during the last two weeks of class. At that time, we review their response sheets and self-evaluation charts and discuss their final grade for the year.

The preceding activities close the year on a most positive note. I learn a great deal about my teaching from their answers. I also find, for example, that many students miss writing the formal letters to me so much that they write them anyway—this always reinforces how that particular form has developed into a means of personal communication between us.

Students Offer Advice

An important suggestion came from my senior writing class: setting deadlines during the quarter so that they would produce at a more even pace. Even though this conflicts with my ideas about allowing each writer the freedom of time during the quarter, I am going to try it next year, because they felt so strongly that people need deadlines. One polished paper will be due during the first quarter at the five-week mark, one at eight weeks, and the last one, plus the letter, at the end of the quarter. Then, during the next three quarters, papers will be due every three weeks, with letters due at the tenth week. This makes sense for everyone, especially for me, since I will not need to do the final reading and grading at the end of each quarter. The students will still be making choices and taking responsibility for their own writing. Why didn't I think of that before?

Another suggestion was that the final portfolio include "a piece of writing that is in stages, from notes to first draft to final draft." Because I knew all the works in progress, I hadn't thought this was necessary, but it does add another dimension, particularly if other people are to read the work in question. Milica commented:

> A portfolio should show off what is done so you can see how a person's work develops. Then even someone else can tell a lot about the writing.

According to their final evaluations, the students recognized their progress in relation to their own needs. Veronica, who came to the United States from Peru only two years before, wrote:

> Now, I sometimes think about my ideas in English, write my first draft in English, use many new words, and know how to separate sentences and paragraphs.

A number of students provided equally telling revelations:

> I used to hate writing but now I see it as a necessary and useful channel for ideas. [Vinny]

> I have learned from writing this piece that it is important to set the tone of the story if I want people to really understand what the main character is feeling. [Jen]

> The whole story changed and improved when I switched to the first person—the main character telling the story from his point of view. [Jeff]

Each of these students expresses a different level of sophistication about writing, based on his or her age and ability. The portfolios have therefore become chronicles of the ways in which students document their growth and take responsibility for analyzing and improving their own writing. Each portfolio I receive expresses the individuality and progress of the writer. I hope that they will come to treasure them as much as I do.

Work Cited

Camp, Roberta. 1989. "Art Propels: Suggestions for Creating Writing Portfolios." Pittsburgh Schools: ETS., n.p.

11 The Empty Space

Linda LaMantia Privette
Centreville High School, Clifton Virginia

Degas' painting, The Rehearsal in the Foyer of the Opera, *is
remarkable at first glance because the principal figure in it, the*
première danseuse, *is off to the extreme left, in a stance of temporary
repose. On the right, the director, with his music book on the lectern
before him, holds his hand up in a gesture of hush and suspense. Some
of the dancers are watching; others are practicing, unconcerned except
with their own exercises, at the bar in the back of the room. Through a
half-open door we glimpse another rehearsal, perhaps more active. But
here, all seems waiting—the mistiness of the mirror at the rear; the
memoried, high gilt ceiling, and even a fragile chair in the foreground,
on which a fan and a pair of slippers have been tossed for the nonce.
Gradually we realize that Degas is not celebrating anything so much
in this picture as the large empty space in the middle of it—the air in
which activity must, in a moment, consummate the dance itself, and
all the technique in demand for it. This space Degas leaves up to us.(1)*

—Roberta T.S. Chalmers, "An Empty Space," unpublished

It seems to me that an empty writing portfolio is like the empty dance floor
in Degas' painting. Both are rich with possibility. The writer, like the dancer,
gives form to that empty space.

Three years ago I experimented with a new portfolio system. At the
beginning of the school year, I gave each of my creative writing students a
manila folder which was quickly named "portfolio." "Portfolio" suggests a
collection of selected but not necessarily polished or finished pieces. The
owner of the portfolio values each of the writings in it for one reason or
another.

The empty space of the inside covers of the portfolio were for the
dialogue that went on between the student writer and me. In the first entry,
the students wrote about their perceived strengths and weaknesses as writers, about topics that were meaningful to them, about forms they wanted
to experiment with, about which conditions helped, and which hindered,
their writing.

I collected the portfolios every other week. I read the contents, read
each student's entry to me, and made my entry a response to three things:

the writings themselves:

"Is there a reason you have used the passive voice?"

"Would a conversation between these two characters make them become more alive?"

the learning context established by that student in her first dialogue entry:

"In your first portfolio entry you said your goal was to polish one good short story. . . . Are you thinking about which one that will be?"

"In September your goal was to write at least one poem and one essay. . . . Has that changed?"

and the student's last dialogue entry:

"You have a fine portfolio this quarter! 'A Parental Storm' shows your understanding and successful use of extended metaphor, the 'necklace tribute' series of poems about family members is a treasure—I hope you will consider polishing those and giving them to those people. You've accomplished all of your goals except one, and this is editing, particularly punctuation. Let's definitely list that as a second quarter priority."

This biweekly exchange continued throughout the four quarters of the school year.

In every teacher's experience, there are moments of epiphany, when she knows something good has happened. I felt this way about the dialogue that evolved through those writing portfolios. The conversation individualized and therefore humanized the entire process of teaching and learning to write. I responded to one human being with a particular set of strengths, weaknesses, joys, fears, experiences, goals. Each folder revealed a story of a writer growing. Because the portfolio provided me with a clear picture of each student's past, present, and future as a writer, I could make connections for the writer that I would not have been able to make were I reading isolated pieces.

At the end of the quarter I scheduled fifteen-minute writing conferences. During this conference, the student and I examined, together, the contents of the portfolio. We reviewed the student's original entry, in which she wrote about her present self as a writer and about her plans and goals as a writer. We discussed to what extent the contents of the portfolio reflected those plans and goals. We assessed the portfolio together and, together, we arrived at a grade.

At the end of the quarter, the students also evaluated the course. One of the questions on the evaluation was, "How did the writing portfolio system help or hinder your writing?" Every student claimed that the process of filling that empty space with dialogue about his or her writing had been very beneficial; many said it contributed more than anything else we did to their development as writers. I know it was one of the best things I have ever done as a teacher.

There was only one problem with my use of writing portfolios: I only used them this way in one class, my creative writing class. I believed my students' writings in my four regular English classes deserved the same attention, but with 125 students every day and only one hour to plan a lesson, the time was simply not available.

The assessment of writing takes time. My students' writing portfolios required hours of reading, reflecting, and then writing—it would have been impossible to give form to that empty space without those hours. The reality is that English/language arts teachers do not deal with simple questions anymore. Years ago, when we *thought* we were teaching writing, the answers were black and white: "Never write an essay in first person. Never use 'you.' See subject-verb agreement in Warriner's, etc." Now that we actually *are* teaching writing, we are dealing with shades of gray. We need to talk and write about what the writer is attempting in the piece, about how the writer can make a passage clearer or more powerful, about why a sentence fragment is just right as the last line. Just as an essay test takes more time to grade than a multiple-choice test, so, too, writing in 1990 takes more time to assess than it did in 1960.

Together, my creative writing students and I gave form and beauty to the empty space of their manila folders—their writing filled it. The process transformed the folder into a portfolio, a collection of writing as art.

12 Interviewing a Portfolio

Bob Ingalls
Mount Vernon High School, Alexandria, Virginia

I "interview" a portfolio as I would a job applicant. I announce my expectations in the form of a rubric, and then give each portfolio the freedom and right to select its best pieces and offer explanations to improve its image. I neither correct nor try to change it. I allow it to talk to me, taking the space it needs. Rather than my planning each step, I let the portfolio direct the interview. I listen and ask questions.

Tell Me Who You Are

I like first for the portfolio to introduce itself to me in a self-assessment, by briefly explaining who its writer is and what that writer thinks about his or her writing. I look for unique interests, opinions, and process steps. These are my first impressions, and they are often important ones. For example, Adam's portfolio introduced itself with confidence:

> This year I have seen my writings improve and my style of writing change. . . . The only thing I don't like about some of my pieces are the small grammatical errors. I would say my writing strengths are the ability to use suspense, action, drama and dialogue (which I recently started). . . . I am very meticulous about my writings and I am very good at writing essays. . . .

Amy's showed her writing preferences:

> I like putting surprises in my writing so you can't really predict what will happen. . . . When I write stories I like to make them very dramatic or emotional. . . . One thing I noticed about myself as a writer is that I like to get my writings the way I like them before I get responses.

Mike's was introspective:

> I see that I have a talent for writing long stories. . . . Some might say a bad habit of mine is daydreaming but I see it as more like a tool that helps me harness the power of my imagination. . . . My weakness I feel is story endings. Somehow I just cannot bring

my stories to a close. When I want to end a story, I automatically think of a new chapter or a sequel. . . . Overall, I write
fairly well. I notice now that ideas to write about come quicker,
and I'm not afraid to write about subjects that I wouldn't even
dream of a year ago.

These brief explanations give me the context to understand and appreciate the writings that follow.

Tell Me about Your Writings

Now that we are past the introductions, we can get specific. The portfolio explains the key things to know about each writing selected, i.e., the
steps taken in the process of writing it, the risks taken, the audience or
purpose chosen, the revision attempts made, the publishing plans or
successes. I like these explanations to be located immediately above or
in front of each piece. This way, I get specific directions to understand
each writing as I read it, which is especially important if I am not the
student's teacher. How else will I know what is being written unless
the portfolio tells me? For example, Mary Chris's portfolio told me about
her first selection:

"Shadows of Death," poem, 10/16/89

I wrote this poem primarily because of a very interesting article
I read on basically the same subject. I thought it would make an
interesting topic for a poem. The only revision made on the draft
of the poem was changing the second to the last stanza.

This portfolio also showed me another writing based on an article. Evi-
dently, the writer works effectively by getting ideas in this fashion, and
she would appreciate knowing if I saw it working for her.

Sometimes the portfolio does not fully trust me. It may take a
moment or two to explain a risky venture—maybe other readers did
not "get the idea" or it is a "first-time" effort. William's portfolio frequently gave such explanations:

"A Question of Romance," poem, 11/89

This was written as if two people, a male and a female, were
arguing on the subject of sex. I know how difficult it is to sustain a relationship 'cause many a girl have let me down throughout my high school years. This writing came from an experience I had with a girl. I was wrong. But it just so happened that
back then I didn't realize it. This poem is unique 'cause it is sort
of a duet. Two people speaking. I love it.

"If I Was a Woman," poem, 11/89

Now I know all men have wondered what it is like to be a woman. Many are probably afraid to admit it. It doesn't mean I'm gay or bisexual. Woman is the best gift God gave to men and all gifts should be appreciated and cherished. The poem takes place as a dream but you wouldn't realize that until the end. Although sequence is not too good, I still put forth good effort.

These explanations give me a context for my comments and evaluation. When student writers speak honestly in their portfolios, I find opportunities for teaching, i.e., telling William about sequencing techniques. I also discover when I should not teach and, instead, just respect a student who loves his writing just as it is.

Sometimes a portfolio needs to tell me about frustration. Kerri's portfolio is frank:

"O.C., The Best," short story, 9/10/89

This writing was a mess. It was much too long and boring so I cut out the majority of the boring parts which ended up cutting my story in half. I polished it by fitting each piece together and then rewriting it neater. Now it's readable.

Portfolios come alive with these explanations. Dawn's portfolio gave out warm invitations to read each piece, with clear indications about their finality:

"My Treasured Gift," poem, 5/89

Somewhere in all of my little treasures, there is a piece about everyone that has ever made an impression on me and my grandmother has many of them. My grandmother died when I was seven, or eight, and she took away from me the one stable thing in my life at the time. This piece was written a while ago and though I did make some revisions, I had a difficult time locating the drafts from the first time I wrote it. Everytime I tried to change it, it got longer and longer but what you see now is the final draft.

"Father," poem, 9/88
"Mother," poem, 9/88

I wrote these pieces at a time in my life when I felt very alone; the time in my life when I would listen to music, visit art galleries, and sit in parks. My parents have never read these and it's probably better that way. They have been revised so many times but they always seem to come back to the same format; it's like the words were meant to fit together and that's the way they're going to stay.

Quite often the portfolio gives me essential information about purpose or intended readers. Laura stated such in the following excerpt:

> **"Amy at the Circus," short story, 10/89**
>
> I changed the first paragraph because Joy suggested to so it wouldn't drag. I also describe the trip there to give a sense of anticipation. Little kids, about the ages of 2–5, I think will enjoy this.

Portfolios encourage student writers to speak with authority about their work. It is a rich moment when student writers discuss their writing honestly and show a mixture of pride and understanding. They learn to speak about their writing at a distance, one step away from tedious revisions and edits. They begin to see connections between the different steps in their work and the various strengths and weaknesses of their portfolio.

Show Me Your Writings

After reading each of these explanations, I read the writing discussed in the portfolio. That way I follow the portfolio directions as laid out for me by the writer. If I were to read all the explanations, I would lose the value of what was said about each individual selection.

The portfolio now faces its toughest task, showing me what it has claimed. I follow along as each portfolio presents a variety of writings, which I appreciate as a result of the explanations. Some portfolios present short pieces, others, long ones. I read Mike's long, semi-autobiographical stories and thought about how he could end them better and some ways in which I could help him. William impressed me with his wondering, and I understood what he was saying in his "duet."

Adam showed me a variety of writings and his "changing style." First, I read his love poem, which was first addressed originally to Lisa and then to Sue. Second, I read an eight-page short story that sounded like a Stephen King version of *The Hobbit*. Next, I read his essay about his favorite book, and then an autobiographical piece explaining his hope of becoming a professional football player. I saw errors, but I also saw an author who was meticulous and stretching his mind.

Sometimes the portfolios do not convince me. I thought Dawn stopped revising one moment too soon, and Kerri was too extreme in her cutting of "O.C., The Best." But these are things I could not know unless the portfolio helped me.

Many students learn the importance of careful preparation; their portfolios direct the interview. During the year, Amy learned to tailor her work, selecting certain portfolio pieces to fit the interview and focusing on different concerns in talking about her writing. When she submitted her work to me each quarter, she made it a point to show evidence of her hard work by including all revised drafts because she knew that would impress me. When she submitted her portfolio for admission to an advanced English class, to a teacher she did not know, she selected pieces, like her abstract poems and literary essays, of the types that she expected to write for the class. I would guess that if she were interviewing for editor in chief of the literary art magazine, she would present writings that would show a sound understanding of many different writing genres.

Discuss Evaluation

Job applicants should come to an interview with their own ideas of what constitutes a fair salary. I expect the same from my student writing portfolios. Using a rubric as a standard, the portfolio and I discuss evaluation. During the year, my students learn that their portfolio grades are often negotiated settlements; this way they know that what they say matters in the final determinations.

I make it clear to my students that my impressions are of what was written but also of what was not. As in any interview, silence is revealing when questions are not answered. This is evident in many ways: final drafts without rough drafts, inability to speak about the writing, or possibly the absence of analytical or essay writing. Since I allow the portfolio to talk and illuminate the work, I am disappointed when it is unable to do so. In the portfolio interview, I am looking for more than the facts; I expect to discover the writer's perspective, opinions, and impressions of writing.

I notice patterns and try to explain what I see. I trust much of what I hear, and suspect what does not seem to gel. I identify what is missing and evaluate the writer's explanation in connection with what she has accomplished. I listen and see if it makes sense with what I see on paper. I am always concerned about the specific pieces, but the explanations are also writing, and they provide evidence of what the writer knows she has done. I learn if the writer is aware enough to repeat successful writing steps, and this helps me to be more certain in my assessment of the portfolio.

I use portfolio interviews because I believe they are fair, but most of all, because they are educational. I like to know if a writer is aware of what she has done, and portfolio interviews make it possible for a writer to talk about her writing. Preparing a portfolio and participating in the interview encourages a student writer to do something that no other part of the writing process does—stand back and study oneself as a writer.

13 Teenage Mutant Ninja Portfolios

Dan Verner
James W. Robinson High School, Fairfax, Virginia

I first seriously considered using portfolios for assessment after a presentation at the 1988 Northern Virginia Writing Project Summer Institute. I was struggling with how to assess my senior English students' writing: I had given up grading individual drafts of writing years ago; I had stressed process, encouraged drafts, revisions, conferences. And yet, at the end of every quarter, I still had to come up with a grade. Portfolios seemed to me to possess the right balance of product and process, and I decided to use portfolios to assess the writings of my students in the 1988–89 school year.

Initially, using Nancie Atwell's (1987) workshop model—in which students and teachers work collaboratively as writers—I broke the writing grade into four parts: participation in writing workshops; an overall portfolio assessment near the end of the quarter; a final "best" paper; and "publishing"—reading a paper aloud or sending a written piece to a publication or contest.

I soon found some difficulties with this scheme: Nancie Atwell could keep up the daily activities of a class; I could not. Maybe she had fewer students or better peripheral vision—in any case, students were receiving credit for working in class who did not deserve it. I had a sense that they didn't, but I could not point to any specific behavior. When I checked, they were on task, but I had the feeling that as soon as my back was turned, they rapidly jumped off.

I also discovered that one folder check per quarter was not enough. I had given the students an assessment sheet with these categories (borrowed from Atwell):

Variety (2 points)

Amount (2 points)

Risk (2 points)

Resources (2 points)

Growth (2 points)

I invited students to share their writing with me when they were ready. Few did—until time for portfolio checks. Even then, some portfolios were filled with poetry; others contained nothing but personal narrative. "What happened to your variety?" I asked. "Huh?" the students said, and they were honestly confused, I think. If there was a deficiency in the portfolios (and I thought, as I always did, that I had communicated expectations clearly), the students had no way to remedy it until the next grading period. Easy enough to fix, I thought. I broke the portfolio assessment in two—a check, once at midquarter, and then again at the end.

I felt better about the portfolio assessment, but I was still dissatisfied. I lacked a clear idea of what or how my students were writing since they were reluctant to share until necessary. And if I lacked that, I could not help them improve.

I shouldn't have been surprised. Most students (like most of us) are self-conscious about their writing, reluctant to share with anyone, resistant to criticism. Clearly, by the end of the first semester, some things needed fixing.

Realizing I could never monitor twenty-five writing processes, I dropped credit for writing workshops and moved my "general impression" of how the students worked into a daily grade, given twice per quarter. I told them this grade would be subjective, and if they could offer evidence to improve my impression of their use of the time, I would take that into account.

The twice-per-quarter portfolio check worked better, but I still felt out of touch. So, I instituted the "Work in Progress" (WIP) grade. At the end of every two writing workshops (in essence, weekly), students were required to show me what they had worked on that week. I could then make comments and suggestions and give credit for satisfactory progress—generally two pages of drafting or an equivalent amount of revision—that was also subjective. These "WIP checks" also showed me what direction to take in conferences with students. I kept a single portfolio check at the end of the quarter to encourage students to keep up their portfolios. The amount, variety, and risk in their writing were easy to see in the WIP checks. Following Atwell's advice, I had no set assignments. Students wrote and produced a variety of work. I decided that students' use of other resources was immaterial to their writing. Some used writing groups; some used pair partners; some wrote alone. (One particularly fine writer stared into space for four or five hours; then she produced twenty to thirty pages of beautifully polished work.) Each grew in writing. In essence, the WIP grade became a kind of floating portfolio assessment check, done seven or eight times throughout the quarter rather than once or twice. Students were involved in self-assessment of their writings as we talked about writing and portfolios; in fact, their assessments of their own work were often harder and more accurate than mine.

I have kept the final paper assignment as is. The students have a sense of closure to their writing, and the grade helps move the writing more toward product. Without it, the work in writing leans more toward process, which might be well in an ideal world of endless revision, but we all know, as writers and students, that there are deadlines and final papers. Students may have drafts of four or five papers per quarter, but may finish only one. The publishing grade is also quite helpful in moving papers along to a public format.

When I began using portfolios to assess writing, I relied almost entirely on the portfolio itself for assessment. I think portfolios and WIPs encourage students to see writing as a process and to take responsibility for their writing. So far, I like using them. Of course, I will change things some more as I go along, but changes like that, I have decided, are part of the process—and the product—of teaching writing.

Work Cited

Atwell, Nancie. 1987. *In the Middle: Writing, Reading, and Learning with Adolescents.* Upper Montclair, NJ: Boynton/Cook.

14 Portfolios: From Negative to Positive

Anne Sharp
Centreville High School, Clifton, Virginia

Writing folders have, in the past, served as protection for me, the teacher. Evidence. My eighth-grade English students' work is on file in case anyone (parents, counselors, etc.) questions or challenges my program or my students' work. "What is Johnny doing in English class? Why, look in his writing folder." Funny. I don't remember one parent asking to see a folder, though. Instead, they seem content talking with me about what we do in class.

Writing folders have also served as protection from "the administration." I began asking students to keep writing folders because I had to. Accountability. Each semester, my former principal collected three student folders from every teacher in every English class. He spent hours reading them and writing detailed letters to teachers, critiquing our writing program based on students' folders. Some comments focused on student writing. Some comments questioned curriculum. Some comments were insightful. Some were downright picky.

I had trouble accepting this folder review. I never knew how to select the folders. Should I pick the absolute best ones so he would think wonderful things were happening with every student? Should I choose a good, an average, and a skimpy folder so he could see the range? Perfection? Accuracy? Why should *I* select folders at all? Why should that be *my* responsibility?

Several years ago, I tried to make this folder review some sort of "learning experience" and attempted to capitalize on it in my classroom. My students often asked, "Why does Mr. S. want to see our writing?" I replied that he was interested in their ideas, that he wanted to know who they were as people and as writers. I told them that he did not often get a chance to talk personally with students because the school was so large. I told them administrative paperwork kept him from getting to know them any other way. Looking at their folders, at their fiction and nonfiction, was a way for him to get to know their lives and imaginations. Yes, I lied.

I am the kind of person who craves integration, and the bureaucracy was fragmenting my curriculum. So I needed to somehow work this folder review into my classroom and have the procedure make sense to my students. There had to be a purpose in the review. The review had to relate to the student or our classroom—not just to "accountability of the English program." I decided, first of all, to have students review and organize their writings. Now, there was an audience besides the teachers—the principal—who was also interested in their brainstorming, drafting, revising, and publishing final products. So we made tables of contents, labeled papers with the purpose of the assignment, and stapled together chronological phases of each writing.

I did not want to decide which three out of twenty-five folders per class to submit, so I gave this responsibility to the students. I asked them to write a persuasive letter convincing me to submit their folder to the principal. Some students asked, "What if we don't want the principal to see our folder, Mrs. Sharp?" I had to respect that request, but they also had to complete the assigned letter. "Well," I replied, "write me a letter persuading me *not* to submit your folder to the principal."

I asked students to leave these persuasive letters in the front of their folders as introductions to their collection. This way, the principal also knew how they felt about their work. Later, I modified the letter assignment so that students wrote directly to the principal—not to me. And I asked the principal to write a note back to the students about what he thought of their writing. "My students are expecting a reply from you," I told him, as I handed him a stack of folders. "They're looking forward to hearing what you think of their writing."

In turn, he wrote a note to each student whose folder he reviewed. He applauded particular pieces and encouraged experimentation with forms. The students enjoyed reading his responses. They saw him step down from his principal's pedestal and comment on movies, books he read, hockey. Some students incorporated his suggestions into their drafts. Some disagreed with his comments. Some shared additional writings with him. For some students, it was the beginning of a dialogue about their writing.

It was also the beginning of a dialogue between teacher and administrator. I worried about handing my principal a stack of folders without any explanation of what had been happening in the classroom. How could he expect to understand the writing without knowing the assignment? How could he understand my program without knowing why and when we wrote the things we did? I did not want him reviewing the folders "cold," so I began by writing a lengthy explanation of what had happened that particular semester. I appended handouts and articles we read. I attached assignment and evaluation sheets. I quoted theory—from teachers, professional writers, myself. And my principal always replied, in writing, to my letters. Sometimes we agreed and sometimes we clashed. And I would drop articles on his desk and invite him to attend workshops and presentations. I figured it was my job to broaden his point of view.

We kept our dialogue a paper one, but we should have talked in person. We should have stepped from behind our paper voices and talked—talked about individual students, class personalities, county curriculum, and my program. We should have talked, but we didn't, and I am not sure why—maybe because of lack of time. Neither my principal nor I made time for another meeting. Maybe we avoided talk because of perceived power. My principal's agenda for writing folders was different from mine. He saw them as evaluation tools for an entire program, while I saw them as records of individual growth. Had the two of us sat down to discuss our agendas, we might have arrived at some common goals and come to a better understanding of the purposes of folders. Then we could have successfully married administration and curriculum. We both could have learned from that. And maybe I would have seen what I see now after writing this article—that my principal had a point. Folders, as I was interpreting them, are not just records of individual growth. They can also be used to assess programs.

15 Portfolio Assessment in the College Writing Classroom

Donald R. Gallehr
George Mason University

Teaching is like most professions—it hands down practices from one generation to the next. So it is that many of us who teach begin by teaching the way we were taught. We remember our better experiences in school and attempt to repeat them.

I have had many good teachers, many of them good English teachers, but the curriculum of the 1940s, 1950s, and early 1960s contained very little writing instruction. Writing was assigned, but rarely taught. Furthermore, the writing assigned in English classes consisted of the literary analysis research paper. The writing of personal essays, stories, poems, and plays was not part of the curriculum.

This dearth of writing was particularly unfortunate for me because I had a strong imagination and would have loved to write stories. Once, when I was in kindergarten, I told my teacher that I had an elephant in the garage. My teacher told my mother and added, "Donald has a very active imagination." I was embarrassed. Rather than channeling my imagination into storytelling and fiction writing, my teachers guided me into writing book reports and research papers. Even my freshman composition course in college restricted students to nonfiction writing, and when I attempted to write about playing high school football, the instructor said it was an inappropriate topic for college.

Consequently, when I began teaching composition, I repeated the strictures handed down to me and did not let my students write personal essays. Over a period of years, however, I, and the profession, began allowing more and more personal writing into the curriculum, and the more we allowed, the more confident students became as writers. Then, in 1978, when I began working with the Northern Virginia Writing Project, I wrote several short stories for my small response group, and I felt as if I had discovered writing for the first time. I used my imagination; I listened to my inner life and expressed it; I watched form emerge as I revised draft after draft; I read my writing to other classroom teachers and used their suggestions to guide me through revision; and I saw myself reflected in the way I wrote. These were the very things I had needed to do since kindergarten. I now teach freshman composition, advanced expository writing, independent writing, and advanced composition, and my teaching reflects my writing experiences in the project. In fact, because I now think and act as a writer, I can help my students to think of themselves as writers.

As a beginning teacher, I had handed down to me not only a method of instruction, but also a system of grading. I am sure you will recognize it. A paper was due each Friday. I usually wrote it on Thursday evening, handed it in on time, and received it back the following week with a grade on it. My semester grade was an average of all the grades I had received during the semester. However, when I switched to treating my students as writers, this method of grading felt uncomfortable and seemed inconsistent. Professional writers did not receive grades—they threw away as much material as they kept, and their reputations grew from the publication of only their best work. Once I recognized the discrepancy between my method of instruction and my method of grading, I searched for a better system of evaluation.

Allow me to digress for a minute. I am not a writer by profession. I am a teacher, paid to teach, to serve the university, and to conduct research. It is within this last category that my own writing is evaluated by the university. How? Through a procedure developed by the many colleges around the country: portfolio assessment.

Each year, my department (and, subsequently, the university) bases my salary on my annual report. Along with my teaching and service to the university, I include a selection of my writings for the year. I omit, for instance, the countless articles in progress, articles that never made it past first draft, as well as stories and poems that are not ready or meant for publication. In other words, I compile a portfolio of my *selected* writings.

I find this system of portfolio evaluation helpful for my writing. I know that when I start a piece, I do not have to include it in my annual report unless I so choose. I also know that if an article is really good, chances are I will be rewarded for it. While I do not have a choice about whether I write—publication is considered part of my job—I do have a tremendous amount of freedom in what I write and when and where I choose to publish.

How is my writing evaluated? The members of the English department salary committee review my work at a meeting in the spring. They sit around a table, annual report in hand. The chair of the department, who also attends this meeting, has notes from a previous meeting I have had with him, to make sure I have left nothing out. The chair, independent of the salary committee, writes his own evaluation, which he submits to the dean of the college. At least one member of the salary committee has read my publications. The first part of the discussion focuses on the merits of my work, and the second part places my accomplishments in the context of the whole department. Once the relative merits of my work have been established, a dollar amount is assigned to determine my new salary, and a recommendation is sent up the line for approval by the dean, provost, president, and board of visitors.

No system of evaluation is perfect, but this peer-review system works well for many of us. The members of the salary committee—the chair, dean, provost, and president—each has his own set of values and view of the university. Reviews occasionally differ, but this system of checks and balances tends to inform rather than restrict; that is, each party represents a different perspective, all of which constitute the university.

I mentioned above that this system of portfolio evaluation works for me as a writer. As a result, I have devised a similar system for my classes. I require my students to write, but within this requirement, they can choose the topic, audience, responders in the class, revision strategies, and much more. They are also free to select from among their works the pieces they want to include in their portfolios. My students know a great deal about the writing of their classmates from working with each other in small groups and from the large-group readings we conduct throughout the semester. This familiarity makes it easier for them to evaluate portfolios.

Early in the semester, I tell my students I want their final portfolios to include the following:

1. A selection of their best work.
2. Drafts to show revision or development over time.
3. One timed writing on a common topic.*

---

* The timed-writing topic I have used most recently is, "Write for forty-five minutes about the changes taking place in your writing." I ask them to use a two-pocket folder, inserting drafts in the left-hand pocket, and the final drafts and prefaces in the right.

4. A preface to each final draft.**

5. A preface to the whole portfolio.

At midsemester, they bring their portfolios to class. We arrange the chairs in a circle and pass the portfolios to the left. They quickly read a half dozen portfolios, and then I ask the students to determine the characteristics of the best and worst selections. I write these on the board, labeling the best category a 4 and the worst a 1. Then I ask for characteristics of a 3 and a 2. We read a few essays aloud to validate the distinctions we are trying to make.

Typically, from a list of fourteen or more characteristics, we narrow the list to items such as the following:

evidence of hard work

evidence of risk taking

the quality of the writings

the appropriate use of resources

variety

carefulness in developing a final draft

the level of difficulty

the degree of interest provided by the topics

We then read another three to five portfolios, this time marking them with a 4, 3, 2, or 1 on a blank page we have attached to the portfolio. With each mark, we fold the page to prevent the next student from seeing the previous marks. Most portfolios receive similar marks. When I see a portfolio receiving a split of two or more (for instance from a 2 to 4, or 1 to 3), I pull that portfolio and we discuss it briefly in an attempt to build consensus.

During this exercise, students learn how to assess holistically. They know they will be using holistic assessment again at the end of the semester, when it will influence their grade for the course, but for now, I give each student a progress grade, my estimate of how well he or she is doing, along with suggestions for improvement.

Between midsemester and the last class, students talk among

** Students use their process logs as prefaces to the midsemester evaluation. By the end of the semester, they revise these process logs for a wider audience and then call them prefaces.

themselves and with me about their portfolios. They ask for advice on what to include, and share their prefaces to get advice for revision. I have found the prefaces to be an invaluable guide in reading the portfolio because the prefaces place each writing in context, showing how the work developed over time. At the end of the semester, for instance, Susan wrote this in her portfolio preface:

> I had no idea I would come up with only four complete essays. For some reason I figured that in fifteen weeks I'd have fifteen complete essays. I guess I forgot about revision. But I'm glad I focused my energy on these four instead of producing lots of bad essays. I acquired a helpful habit of meticulous revision.

Tom, in his portfolio preface, showed that he was pleased with his work and revised each piece extensively. From a comment he made in class, I knew he had not revised in previous courses because his first drafts were sufficient to earn him respectable grades:

> When writing for this class I did the best I could to deal with topics that had been on my mind for a long time, such as racism, censorship, and the destruction of nature. I also tried to take everything I wrote way above the level of anything I had written before. I feel that I have succeeded on both counts. . . .
>
> With the exception of "Fear," everything included here is something that I have wanted to write for a long time, but up until this semester I never had the time, or the motivation. Actually getting that stuff on paper after all the time I've spent thinking about it was a tremendous relief to me. "Fear," as I say in the preface to that work, came about at a moment of desperation, but it turned into what I think is an excellent paper. . . .
>
> Of the four papers you see here, only one, "A Youthful Perspective on Rock," went through less than three revisions. The others, "Growing Up White in a White World," "Fear," and "August in the Shenandoah," were revised several times each. I believe that what you see here is a sample of my best writing. It is certainly, by far, the best work I have done to date.

During the last class of the semester, we read the portfolios using the same procedures we devised at midsemester. We warm up by reading three or four portfolios, then read another two or three, mark them, and add several sentences on "Why I gave it this mark." Each is read by at least two students, and if the split between marks is wide, I give it to a third and sometimes even a fourth. When we are sure that all portfolios have received at least two marks of the same number, we return the portfolios to the owners, who have the last word by adding a final note to their portfolios.

Not all students are pleased with the marks or the reasons for the marks. Cassie, for instance, received 3's along with this comment: "I can tell you put a lot of work into this and I love your writing style. You have a great gift for description and your control of time is really neat." In response, Cassie wrote:

> Of course, I like these comments because they are nice; however, I feel like maybe they are giving me a 3 because in order to give a 2, one would have to have a pretty bad portfolio. So, I feel that I am being patronized, in a way. I don't feel that these are sincere comments because if I receive a 3 out of 4, obviously something is missing in my writing, and I would like to know what that is. I guess people are afraid to tell me what's wrong— or maybe they just don't know.

I tell my students that I often find myself in agreement with the marks of their classmates. I know them and their work well. In most instances, the marks given by the students are consistent with the grades I give them for the course (4's = A's; 3's = B's; and so on). In Cassie's case, however, I disagreed with the student marks (3's) and wrote, "Perhaps there was nothing wrong. I agree with their comments but would have given you 4's. So, I'm giving you an A for the semester. You've done well."

Portfolio assessment is philosophically consistent with the other parts of my writing course: It recognizes and rewards revision, maintains realistically high standards, and places me in a position of guiding their writing with minimal evaluation—until the very end of the course, when they become co-evaluators. Portfolio evaluation also prepares my students to submit work for publication. They learn how to select their best pieces, and through the sometimes conflicting evaluations of their classmates, they glimpse the differing opinions of editors.

16 What Student Portfolios Are Teaching Us

Laura Brady
West Virginia University

Christopher Thaiss
George Mason University

N ow we had a problem. Back in 1981, we had proposed this wonderful course for upper-division students—"Advanced Composition." We envisioned it giving force to the university's new com-
mitment to writing across the curriculum. First, it would be structured
to relate directly to the writing that students would be doing in their
majors. Second, it would be required of all students: a clear sign of the
university's belief that writing was important throughout a student's
college career, not just a two-semester hurdle in the freshman year.

So we fought the battles in the faculty senate against those who
claimed that juniors and seniors could not fit into their schedules any
course other than a "major" one. We marshaled our arguments and our
supporters, and we won.

By spring 1988, we had won so handily that we had about sixty
sections per semester of advanced composition and about 1,400 students enrolled. We had almost more sections than we could hire quali-
fied faculty to teach. Worse, we had a waiting list of 200 students per
semester. Waiting students clamored, sometimes loudly, for sections.
As an alternative to waiting, many complained to the director of composition, asking why this course was required. "I'm a senior," they said.
"I've gotten through my writing this far. Do I really need another writing course?"

Moreover, teachers were reporting to us that, indeed, some of their
students were too good for the course: "Isn't there a way they can test
out?" No, there wasn't. By "test," we imagined (actually failed to imagine anything other than) a one-shot, timed, writing sample in response
to a suitable topic: exactly what we used to test those who wanted to be
exempted from first-year composition, and exactly the sort of exam ETS
uses for the same purpose. How could such a test account for the varied skills, plus the knowledge of process, the sense of audience, the

deftness at research, that we hoped we were nurturing in advanced composition?

By spring 1988, it was too late to keep asking this rhetorical question. We needed a valid way to assess the skills of students who desired to be exempted from the requirement, or whose teachers wanted to encourage them to seek exemption. From our reading of the recent literature on assessment, we hit on portfolios. Portfolios would allow us

> to validate the student's breadth of writing experience—diverse audiences, form, purposes;
>
> to assess a range of skills, from mechanical competence, to stylistic versatility, to the ability to analyze and synthesize data;
>
> to escape the artificial limitation imposed by the pressure of time and by the lack of opportunity for feedback and revision;
>
> to accommodate writers who composed best on the word processor (we do not have PCs available in the department for testing situations).

Further, by requiring portfolios, we believed we would discourage those who might be willing to "take a shot" at a timed essay but who did not want to put the time into compiling a varied sample of their earlier work (or who cared so little about their writing that they had not kept copies of their previous work). We wanted to be sure that the people whose proficiency we were validating really could do the many tasks that the teacher of the course would expect over the semester.

Portfolio Content

We wanted portfolios that would represent the range of writing practiced in advanced composition, as well as the range of writing we could expect the student to have done after two or three years at the university. In other words, we wanted variety without too much bulk. In the guidelines we gave to students, we asked for at least three short pieces (three to five pages each) that demonstrated the following aspects of writing:

> a range of audiences and purposes;
>
> a mastery of analysis, argumentation, and persuasion;
>
> varied organizational strategies;
>
> logical coherence and evidence in support of arguments.

We also asked for one longer writing sample (eight to fifteen pages) that demonstrated knowledge of research techniques relevant to the student's major field of study, practice in the integration and citation of sources, analytical reasoning, and logical coherence. Further, we asked for copies of papers without grades or comments, because we did not want to be biased by a previous teacher's assessment. Like everyone else, we knew that we were prone to focus on the evaluation rather than the text itself.

The Timed "Process" Essay

Not long into our discussion of portfolios, we realized the one advantage of the timed essay: its ability to verify that the student and the writer were the same person. How could our student writers prove that they had indeed written what was in their portfolios? We decided to add another part to the process: a two-hour, timed essay written in a proctored setting. This, at least, would allow us to compare the verified with the unverified, so that we could question marked differences. We spent a good deal of time seeking "good questions" to ask on such a test. Eventually, we settled on a task that we hoped would tell us more than just whether the writer was truthful:

> Refer to two pieces included in your portfolio. Write about each. Explain your motivation to write the piece; describe your process of collecting information (sources used, problems encountered in the research); describe your process of drafting and revising, including, for example, your favorite tricks for getting started, for organizing your work, for understanding your audience, for getting feedback on your writing as it progresses.

This task might let us see the writer as writer, the process that lay behind the pieces in the portfolio. While taking a course, a student reveals to the teacher whether or not she is proceeding; even portfolios do not do this, unless they include drafts and/or students' comments on their processes. We could not hope that students had kept drafts of papers written perhaps a year or two earlier, yet we wanted to assess, if possible, their knowledge of themselves as writers, their ability to think, impromptu, about how the "products" in the portfolio had taken shape.

The Three Steps in the Assessment

Procedurally, the timed essay would come after the portfolio had been submitted and after a member of our composition committee had done a cursory review of the portfolio. The first review focused on mechanical competence:

> Aside from a very few errors in usage, syntax, punctuation, and spelling, could the student comfortably follow the conventions of Standard Edited English?

If so, we would invite the student to write the timed portion. If not, we would counsel the student about the need to take the course. For those who advanced to step two, we would evaluate the "process essay" with attention to these factors:

> understanding of the "process terms" (drafting, audience, revision, etc.), as shown in how the student wrote about them;
>
> the amount of specific detail in the description of each process (Does the writer recognize distinctions in audience, purpose, and language from one task to another?);
>
> organization, syntax, and other mechanical features.

The student who adequately met these criteria would advance to the third, and final, step—the assessment of the portfolio by a faculty member in the major department. Why include this step? Why not trust our own judgment?

Assessment of the Portfolio by the Major Department

When college faculty look to the English department for assessment of writing proficiency, they ignore the fact that assessment of writing is occurring whenever a teacher evaluates a piece of student writing, whether a quiz, an exam, a lab report, a computer program, a literature review, a case analysis, a treatment plan, etc. Whether or not the evaluator looks at such conventionally "Englishy" features as spelling, usage, and syntax, the writing is still evaluated—for how clearly data is presented, how well a point is argued, how well the writer understands the terms of the subject matter. Those of us who observe writing across the curriculum know that every discipline has somewhat differing standards, plus its own jargon. If we really believe, as we tell our students, that what we should write changes as our purpose, our audience, and our data change, then we have to admit any one individual's inadequacy to evaluate all relevant features of a cross-disciplinary portfolio.

So, when we designed the portfolio plan, we included step three: assessment by a member of the major department. We figured that cases would occur when we would doubt our ability to judge unfamiliar formats and strange technical terms; we wanted to be able to ask the assistance of a person who would be comfortable with the writing.

Moreover, we saw step three as a tangible way to keep departments thinking about student writing. We knew that some faculty members might object, arguing that we in English were just passing the buck by "imposing" on them the burden of advanced composition portfolio evaluation. But we were willing to risk this ire in exchange for getting the message out that we were not buck-passing, but rather, giving credit to the expertise of those who could better judge in certain situations. We also knew that we had done enough seed work in writing-across-the-curriculum theory during the past ten years to ensure a largely favorable response.

Our Ideas in Practice

Our portfolio system has been in place for about a year now. So far, we have only received about a dozen portfolios in all, and no more than two from any given program. Of these, we have exempted eight students (75 percent) from their advanced composition requirement. While we are surprised that more students have not submitted portfolios, several factors may account for the relatively low numbers: the portfolio exemption is not listed in the undergraduate catalog; faculty and advisors are not yet fully aware that the option exists; the process requires more time and effort to compile than some students want to give. (We regularly spend time explaining the exemption process to students, but little more than half of these conversations result in portfolios.)

Not only have we received fewer submissions than we anticipated, but our evaluation process also differs from our original plan. The three-part evaluation process—the initial review of the portfolio, the timed essay, and a second reading by a faculty member in the student's major department—has, in practice, become a two-step process. Instead of a cursory review by a member of the composition committee, the portfolio receives a thorough reading that accounts for factors such as focus, development, and organization, in addition to mechanical competence; the reader also looks for a sense of audience and purpose as revealed by details, amount and type of evidence, diction, syntax, and so forth. As readers, we found that it was impossible to look only at the surface features of the writing and not notice or comment on larger patterns. Because we also teach advanced composition, we knew from experience what types of writing practice the course offered, and thought we were able to advise students on whether they would benefit from the requirement.

Despite our good intentions of involving them, faculty from other departments have (so far) been quite willing to accept our evaluations without even reading the portfolios. Upon asking for second readers from other departments, we have found that our colleagues do not see the need for another reader. They have told us that they would look at the same things—focus, coherence, development, stylistic and mechanical features. One colleague said that because he had not taught the advanced composition course and the members of the composition committee had, he preferred to let us make the call on whether the student needs the required course.

Surprisingly, we have not seen the need for a second reader, either. At least not so far. We have yet to read a portfolio that seems to call for specialized expertise on the part of the reader; none of the samples we've read have presented unusual formats or strange technical terms. This may be because almost all of the portfolios to date have been from the humanities and social sciences: anthropology, criminal justice, education, government, philosophy, political science, English, European studies. Even the two portfolios we received from outside these areas—one from nursing and the other from psychology—presented standard expository essays that did not require specialized knowledge to understand the content. The nursing major presented a case study (a form of narrative), a problem-solving analysis, and an explanatory essay on teaching nutrition to a specific group of patients. The psychology major's portfolio consisted of papers she had written for her required English literature classes and one case-study narrative from a course in her major. When we do receive portfolios that include highly technical samples, or writing for a highly specialized audience, we will need our colleagues' expertise. Until then, we are able to process the student appeals more quickly with one reader, even though we are sacrificing the involvement of faculty from beyond the English department.

Let us give you a couple of examples of how the system is working currently. If a writer appears to already possess the skills practiced in advanced composition, the evaluation can provide the students with some feedback on the specific strengths and patterns revealed in the writing portfolio because, unlike other systems of evaluation, the portfolio does reveal patterns. The evaluator can see how a writer's style develops and changes over time, and in relation to different subjects or contexts. For example, after reading the process essay that accompanied a strong and varied portfolio, the reader could point to passages that demonstrated the writer's ability to balance considerations of audience and purpose with decisions about the content and style. In another instance, the portfolio revealed the writer's understanding of his processes and choices as a writer; his process essay pointed to the same patterns that the reader had observed in the writing samples: deliberate use of rhetorical tropes (such as questions and self-reflective comments) to involve the reader, as well as the use of definitions and background information to increase the reader's general understanding of the subject before focusing attention on one specific aspect of it.

Similarly, for students who either do not want to take the advanced writing course or are unsure whether they need to, the portfolio lets the reader both evaluate and advise by looking at the patterns which several, varied samples reveal. A student majoring in psychology submitted a portfolio at the beginning of the fall semester. She was already enrolled in a section of advanced composition, but wasn't sure whether she needed the course. In all of the courses she had completed within her major, she consistently received grades of A and B. With only twenty-two more credits needed to graduate, she wanted advice on whether she would gain anything from the advanced writing requirement. We recommended that she submit a portfolio of her strongest work. What follows is an excerpt from the comments made by the initial reader—a member of the English department faculty:

> I am particularly concerned by one recurrent pattern: the writer makes assertions without offering specific support. This indicates problems in development and argumentation; it also accounts for problems in maintaining a clear sense of purpose since the essays do not show how the writer reached her conclusions.

The reader concluded by recommending that the student take advanced composition to develop stronger research and documentation skills, and to increase her awareness of how audience, purpose, content, and style are interrelated.

Some students take the initiative to include a cover letter that explains why they are petitioning to be exempted from advanced composition, what they view as their strengths, and why they have included the particular pieces gathered in the portfolio. This, in addition to the self-reflective piece, which we ask the students to write as the piece of timed writing for the portfolio, allows the student to initiate the review of her own work. The student's process essay is frequently the deciding factor on a borderline portfolio that is teetering between a "pass" (which exempts the student from advanced composition) and a "no pass" (which requires the student to take the course). The process essay provides the basis for a type of written dialogue between the student and the faculty evaluator.

Revelations from the Process Essays

Thus far, the process essays have exceeded our expectations in their usefulness. Thankfully, we have not found any suspicious discrepancies between the competence of the portfolio and that of the process piece. Nor have we found, not surprisingly, process essays that noticeably exceed the portfolios in fluency, clarity, or correctness. Yes, we do find, as we would expect, that the essays bear the marks of initial drafts:

> the first few paragraphs often show the writer groping for a focus;
>
> there are a few uncaught errors in spelling and syntax;
>
> in striving for clarity of thought, the writers recast ideas in different words, and thus are sometimes repetitious;
>
> logical connections between ideas are not always explicit.

But more than anything else, the process essays teach us. They open to us the world behind the portfolio. In a way, they teach us how to read the portfolios. In one instance, one of us had reacted unfavorably to a government major's portfolio that had seemed politically one-sided, the arguments predictable and superficial. Although the writer's syntax was sophisticated, his vocabulary varied, we questioned his overall writing strength. The process essay showed us a very thoughtful writer, whose portfolio had been substantially composed of news analyses and research reports he had written as part of his job—as a writer for a political action organization! The essay showed us his awareness of subtle shifts in audience and purpose from piece to piece, and led us to see more in the portfolio than we had first been able to see.

Beyond this, the essays demonstrate the uniqueness of the writer. They speak with different voices; they reveal a range of favorite techniques. One writer, a decision science major, refers to herself in the third person and uses formal vocabulary, as if she were writing a report for the agency at which she works. She sets up a writing task in formal phases:

> From information provided during orientation and interview processes, Ms. _____ learned that this report was intended for management, functional personnel, and computer personnel. Thus, the Sizing Study had to be both a high-level presentation of the analytical results and an in-depth presentation of the specific analytical tools, techniques, and information.

Another, a criminal justice major, explains his technique by describing his past and his feelings about it:

> Being an avid reader to begin with, it was easy for me to collect research material on a radically new approach to handling juvenile offenders, which was the topic of my "Integrative Paper #3." For years I have been caught up in the mechanism of a system that does not work. Therefore, prior to drafting my paper, I spoke with numerous Assistant United States Attorneys and got their viewpoints.

A third, an anthropology major, describes her feelings about her research material and how those feelings influenced her process:

> After reading and listening to the lyrics of the songs, I found them to be truly offensive. It was difficult to discuss specific examples of vulgarity and I was worried that it would offend any readers other than my sociology professor. Concerned about this, I asked my mother to read it. After this, I edited and revised certain parts, which was difficult, because I did not want to take out too much information.

The uniqueness of the writers notwithstanding, the process essays sustain our belief, nurtured by twenty years of research by many people in many contexts, that successful writers think about variables: audience, purpose, format, etc. Moreover, they are comfortable with making choices and making changes. They approach this process deliberately, often very systematically. When asked to write about it, off the cuff, they can, in detail. This is not to say that all these writers are conscious every moment of the choices they make—we would like to probe this question more deeply with our portfolioists—but their comfort with process lets them write easily about those aspects—planning, audience, feedback, revision—that are consistent from person to person. The writers whose portfolios do not succeed with us (very few, as we have noted) write essays with nothing like the detail and personality suggested by the preceding samples. They write about where they research for information, but the statements on audience, feedback, and revision are sketchy.

Although we had originally intended the timed essay to give us no more than some proof of the honesty of the portfolioists, we discovered avenues of insight into the writers, plus a tool to help us read the portfolios. Beyond this, we believe we have stumbled upon a rich vein for further research. The "portfolios plus" (portfolio plus process essays) gives us a starting point for further study of the great variety of environments in which these writers work.

What Next?

In addition to integrating the evaluation process more fully into all the disciplines, we in English need to consider the implications the portfolio system has for our own department, our own curriculum. If we believe that student work should be evaluated holistically, on the basis of several pieces of writing that reveal patterns and growth, shouldn't we reconsider conventional approaches to grading? Why not respond to work in progress, and let the student decide when it is ready for final evaluation? Such a shift in grading practices would have us evaluate all of a student's writing for the semester as a whole body of work compiled over the course of a semester. While it would mean a larger stack of papers, it would require only a little more time—assuming that the instructor has seen everything at some point in the composition and revision process that took place during the term.

Some of our faculty already use portfolios for evaluating course work. They report that this holistic approach to grading offers advantages similar to those we have noticed in the exemption portfolios: The students have more authority, as well as more responsibility, for judging when their work is ready for evaluation, and most develop a clearer sense of what was or was not working well for them as writers; the teacher-evaluators can begin their discussions of each student's work with that student's sense of herself as a writer.

The concept of portfolios has led to discussions among our faculty about ways of responding to student writing. The portfolio approach will be the focus of one of our brown-bag lunches, where faculty meet to share teaching ideas. Specifically, the concepts of portfolios will let us examine our goals and methods for responding to student writing. If one of our goals as teacher-evaluators is to increase students' awareness of themselves as writers, then the "portfolio plus" approach (writing plus self-reflective analysis) offers a unique way to initiate a dialogue between teachers and students, which should increase both sides' understanding of the process of writing and evaluation.

Ideally, any sort of assessment should do more than test specific skills or knowledge; assessments should also help us learn about ourselves, our strengths, and our needs. We know that we as readers have already learned from the portfolio process. We look at evaluation and assessment in a new way, conscious of the assumptions we carry with us as readers, conscious of the value of listening to students' explanations of their context and their choices, and conscious of the choices we make as teachers and evaluators when we present strategies for reading and writing. As a result, we are examining our classroom grading approaches, renewing our beliefs in teaching students about the ongoing processes of reading and writing, and revising our assumptions about how to gauge writing competency. We hope that the portfolios (and our courses) also increase the students' awareness of themselves as writers, and of their relationship to a range of audiences reading with varied purposes.

Editor

Kent Gill has led a long and productive career in education and public service. For thirty years, he taught English and history at Holmes Junior High School in Davis, California, from which he is now retired. He is currently a volunteer, teaching writing, at Black Butte School, Camp Sherman, Oregon. He took his B.A. from the University of Colorado in 1950; his M.Ed. from the University of Oregon in 1954; and a Certificate of Advanced Study from Harvard University in 1969. Among the many positions he has held in education are teacher-consultant, Area III English Project, California, 1963–68; teacher-consultant, Bay Area Writing Project, 1976; various roles with the Area III Writing Project, California; a member of the Writing Development Team, California Assessment Project, 1985–88. He is co-author (with Jackie Proett) of *The Writing Process in Action* (NCTE, 1986) and editor of the *Area III Third Report* (1966). He served as chair of the NCTE Committee on Classroom Practices, 1987–92. He has also served as president of the Sierra Club, 1974–76, and mayor of Davis, California, 1966–68.

Contributors

Carole Ackerson Bertisch is the English facilitator for Rye Neck High School, Mamaroneck, New York. She developed and implemented a writing program for the district and has conducted inservice workshops for teachers throughout Westchester County, specializing in writing process, reading instruction, and the value of portfolios in all grades, K–12. While on sabbatical, she was the recipient of a postgraduate research grant at Lehman College, which led to her article, "Creation of a Community," published by the Teachers Network News, Harvard University, the New York City Writing Project, and the *CSSEDC Quarterly* (now *English Leadership Quarterly*). She is a regular presenter at conferences in New York.

Laura Brady is assistant professor of English at West Virginia University, where she teaches composition and women's studies. She previously taught at George Mason University, and was a teacher-consultant for the Northern Virginia Writing Project. She has published in *Computers & Composition* and *Computers in the Humanities* and is a member of the editorial board for *Women and Language*. She is currently working on a book-length study of collaborative authorship. She regularly presents at CCCC, NCTE, and regional conferences.

Marylyn E. Calabrese, former English department chair at Conestoga High School, Berwyn, Pennsylvania, has taught high school English for most of her career. Her journal articles and conference presentations have focused on the theory and practice of teaching revision, responding to student writing, and writing center research. Her current work as a business writing consultant deals with issues of workplace literacy for both adult employees and for students preparing to enter the work force.

Lela M. DeToye is assistant professor in the School of Education at Southern Illinois University at Edwardsville. She teaches language arts methods and children's literature at the graduate and undergraduate levels. In addition to her teaching duties, she directs the Mississippi Valley Writing Project. She has served on several NCTE committees and presents regularly at local, state, and national conferences.

Margo A. Figgins is assistant professor of English education at the University of Virginia, director of the UVA Writer's Workshop for young writers, and co-director of the Central Virginia Writing Project. Also a well-known poet, she teaches in Poets-in-the-Schools programs throughout the state, sponsored by the Virginia Commission for the Arts. Her poems have appeared in various magazines and journals, among them *Iris, Artemis,* and *Language Arts*.

Donald R. Gallehr is associate professor of English at George Mason University, director of the Northern Virginia Writing Project, and co-director of the National Writing Project. He regularly teaches advanced nonfiction writing to undergraduates, teaching-of-writing courses to graduate students, and workshops in writing to adults in business and government. His articles have appeared in National Writing Project newsletters and *The Quarterly*. The working title of his nonfiction writing text is *The Practice of Writing*.

Bob Ingalls is the language arts department chair at Mount Vernon High School, Alexandria, Virginia, and an assistant director of the Northern Virginia Writing Project. He has taught high school English and speech for fourteen years, and has worked as a Writing Project teacher-consultant in Virginia and metropolitan Washington, D.C., for the past seven years. In addition to articles about his classroom practices, he has written several articles about his school's four-year portfolio study, recently collaborating with Joyce Jones on "There's a Lot of Things You Learn in English You Can't Really See," published in *The Quarterly* of the National Writing Project and Center for the Study of Writing and Literacy. He makes presentations regularly at Writing Project sites and occasionally at state and national conventions.

Robert W. Keiper is professor of secondary education at Western Washington University, where he teaches general secondary methods, conducts microteaching sessions, and supervises student teachers. He has taught K–12 dramatic arts and middle school and high school language arts in rural, suburban, and urban settings. Recognized for his publications, he is also known nationally for his "Teacher as Actor" workshops, which he has conducted at various national meetings in the United States and Canada and at inservices for educators in the public, private, and higher education settings.

Betty McWilliams is a twelfth-grade English instructor at Waco High School, Waco, Texas. She has also taught high school Spanish. In addition to twenty-six years of high school teaching, she recently taught business English at McLennan Community College. She is a freelance writer for *Discover Waco* magazine and makes presentations at Central Texas Writing Project sites and Baylor University TAIR conferences.

Elaine Murphy teaches humanities and honors English courses at Ursuline Academy, Dallas, Texas. She has taught English at all levels from junior high through undergraduate and has also served as a college writing center coordinator and a journalism advisor. She has published several articles in *English Journal* and has presented at NCTE and other language arts conventions at the state and national levels.

Robert J. Nistler is assistant professor of reading and language arts education at the University of North Texas. He has taught upper intermediate grades in elementary schools, served as an elementary school reading specialist, and worked as a coordinator of school district compensatory programs. He recently completed a three-year collaborative program in which he worked with elementary teachers interested in changing their approaches to literacy instruction.

Linda LaMantia Privette is department chair and teacher of English at Centreville High School, Clifton, Virginia. She is a teacher-consultant for the Northern Virginia Writing Project and is editor in chief of the *Northern Virginia Writing Project Newsletter.*

D. R. Ransdell is currently teaching first-year composition at the University of Arizona, while working toward a doctorate in rhetoric and composition. She will have another article on pedagogy appearing in a 1993 issue of *English Language Teaching.*

Anne Sharp is a journalism teacher at Centreville High School, Clifton, Virginia, where she is also sponsor of the student newspaper, *The Centreville Sentinel.* She has taught English and creative writing at both the middle school and high school levels and is a teacher-consultant for the Northern Virginia Writing Project.

Joseph E. Strzepek is associate professor of English education in the Curry School of Education at the University of Virginia and director of the Central Virginia Writing Project. With co-author Robert Small, he wrote *A Casebook for English Teachers: Dilemmas and Decisions.* He has published book chapters, articles, and poems in *Four Psychologies Applied to Education, Observation Methods in the Classroom, Focus: Teaching English Language Arts,* the *Virginia English Bulletin, Tennis,* and *Poems for Summer: Seasonal Poetry.* He has taught English in grades 7–12, consulted with school divisions throughout Virginia, and regularly given presentations at NCTE and state conventions.

Christopher Thaiss directs the composition and writing-across-the-curriculum programs at George Mason University, where he is associate professor of English. Active in the development of cross-curricular writing in schools and colleges since 1978, Thaiss also coordinates the National Network of Writing Across the Curriculum Programs and works with teachers in elementary, middle, and high schools through the Northern Virginia Writing Project. Books he has written or edited include *Writing to Learn: Essays and Reflections; Speaking and Writing, K–12* (with Charles Suhor); *Language Across the Curriculum in the Elementary Grades;* and a composition textbook, *Write to the Limit.* Current projects include a composition anthology (*A Sense of Value*) and a book on youth baseball.

Dan Verner is an English and creative writing teacher at James W. Robinson High School, Fairfax, Virginia. He has published several articles locally, related to the teaching of writing, and given presentations for local conferences on using narrative in the classroom and music to encourage writing. He has had several poems published in *English Journal* and is a teacher-consultant with the Northern Virginia Writing Project.

Beverly Wilkins has taught English and history for twenty years. In 1992, she received her M.S. Ed. in curriculum and instruction, with an endorsement in gifted and talented education, from Baylor University. In addition to her teaching assignment at Midway Middle School, Waco, Texas, she is a freelance writer, specializing in historical topics. She is also a National

Writing Project fellow and conducts writing workshops for local school districts. She has made several presentations at the Texas Association for the Improvement of Reading (TAIR) conferences and Baylor University's National Writing Project.

Gail M. Young is a language arts teacher at Hillsboro High School, Hillsboro, Oregon. She has also taught in Tucson, Arizona, and Morristown, New Jersey. Her current assignment combines teaching language arts in the special education department with teaching a sophomore interdisciplinary world studies block in the International High School Program. She serves on the steering committees of the International High School and the school improvement team. She is also a graduate of the Oregon Writing Project. This is her first published work.

Titles in the Classroom Practices in Teaching English Series

NCTE began publishing the Classroom Practices series in 1963 with *Promising Practices in the Teaching of English*. Volumes 1–16 and Volumes 18–20 of the series are out of print. The following titles are available through the NCTE *Catalog:*

Vol. Title

17. *How to Handle the Paper Load* (1979)

21. *Literature—News That Stays News: Fresh Approaches to the Classics* (1985)

22. *Activities to Promote Critical Thinking* (1986)

23. *Focus on Collaborative Learning* (1988)

24. *Talking to Learn* (1989)

25. *Literature and Life: Making Connections in the Classroom* (1990)

26. *Process and Portfolios in Writing Instruction* (1993)

27. *Ideas for the Working Classroom* (1993)